MW00423690

# What If Everyone Lived Next Door to JESUS?

*And Other Meditations from a Missionary's Heart*

## GARY STONE

**HANNIBAL BOOKS**
www.hannibalbooks.com

Published by
HANNIBAL BOOKS
PO Box 461592
Garland, Texas 75046-1592
www.hannibalbooks.com
1-800-747-0738

Copyright 2008
All Rights Reserved

Printed in the United States of America
by Lightning Source, LaVergne, TN
Cover design by Dennis Davidson
Back cover photo by Lindsay E. Stone

Unless otherwise noted, all Scripture quotations are taken from
the Revised Standard Version of the Bible

ISBN 978-1-934749-14-2
Library of Congress Control Number: 2008932716

TO ORDER ADDITIONAL COPIES, SEE PAGE 301.

Have you ever wanted to sit down with a missionary and hear his or her stories? Then look no further than this book. It will feel as if Gary Stone is sitting at your kitchen table talking directly to you. Let me give you fair warning: you may let out a laugh or you may even shed a tear. But one thing is certain: you will be inspired. Ordinary stories are told and heard. But good stories are experienced and remembered. *What if Everyone Lived Next Door to Jesus?* is a collection of good stories.

> *David M. Blanton*
> *Sr. Pastor, Southside Baptist Church*
> *Spartanburg, S.C.*
> *Former IMB missionary to Ecuador*

*What if Everyone Lived Next Door to Jesus?* is truly outstanding! It is the kind of story that makes you laugh, cry and praise the Lord all at once. It's full of insight into human nature.

> *Dr. Harry Byrd*
> *Author and retired IMB missionary to Guatemala*

Gary has a unique way of relating to readers from teenagers to adults ... . It feels like your best friend is sharing with you. He grabs attention and motivates readers to live a missions lifestyle.

> *Cindy Skelton*
> *South Carolina Woman's Missionary Union*
> *GA Consultant/Camp Program Director*

I felt like we'd had a face-to-face visit after I read your story "To Dream Again." May God save us all from spending too much time looking into the mirror instead of up at the stars!

> *Robert Hooker*
> *Evangelism Consultant, Collegiate Ministry,*
> *BGCT*
> *Former IMB missionary to Canada, Guatemala*
> *and Mexico*

# TABLE OF CONTENTS

# STORY LIST

# PREFACE

THIS BOOK WAS BORN out of our life and work as Christian missionaries. Missions has been our family's passion for most of our lives. We have had the privilege of serving in the United States, Ecuador, Australia and Guatemala for more than 25 years, and it is with thankfulness that we offer to you now the stories and experiences of our hearts.

It is with deep love and appreciation
that I dedicate this book to my brother

THE REVEREND STEVE STONE

and to my wife, daughter and son

LILY, LINDSAY AND WILLIAM STONE

who have shared the journey with me
and have made my life
brighter and better in every way.
Were it not for their love and patience,
this book would never have come to be.

It is also with profound admiration
that I would like to express my gratitude for

ALL OF MY CHRISTIAN MISSIONARY COLLEAGUES

who are making a difference around the world
for the cause of Christ.
May others always have good stories to tell
because you went ... and because you cared.

CHAPTER ONE

Recognizing the Brokenness Inside

## 1.1
## Morgan's Creek

*... Now hope that is seen is not hope.*
*For who hopes for what he sees?*
– Romans 8:24b

IN THE DEEP RECESSES of my heart there resides a memory that is brighter than most. It is a memory of my brother and me playing in a country creek.

As the cool water runs over us, we anchor ourselves among the rocks with one hand and eat watermelon with the other. We spit seeds at one another and laugh. Occasionally we have to stop and wipe our faces clean with the creek water. We splash each other, sing, tell jokes and take sheer delight in our creek as though it were the Amazon. This is our "vacation," and we are thoroughly delighted with it.

During the 1960s when I was growing up, not everyone was fortunate enough to "go on vacation." To tell the truth, some of us didn't really know what one was. I still chuckle at the scene in the movie "Forrest Gump" where little Forrest asks where his father is. Mrs. Gump gives him the same answer she gives to everyone else who asks: She replies that Mr. Gump is "away on vacation."

"What is a vacation?" Forrest asks his mother.

"A vacation," his mother tells him, "is when you go away and don't ever come back."

Somehow vacations just don't seem that appealing when you put it that way! In our little mill town of Williamston, South Carolina, vacations were activities for families wealthier than ours. While my brother and I often heard others talking about taking trips to exotic places that seemed as far away as the moon, we didn't have a clue as to how they arranged it! To us, vacation was when the cotton mill where our parents worked closed down for the week of the Fourth of July and all the employees got to stay home.

Every year our father would put on his overalls (without a shirt … for vacation) and lie in a hammock on our carport for most of the week. We, in turn, would play football or baseball and do the same things that we always did in the summer, and that wasn't bad. Not bad at all!

"I can't wait for Fourth of July week!" my friends at school would say. "We're going to Myrtle Beach!" Others would head to Florida or go visit grandma in Georgia, or head to Six Flags, etc. I must confess that I did often feel a little jealous that these kids were getting to explore the ends of the Earth while we stayed on the mill hill.

When we would ask our father where we were going, he would usually grin and say that we were going to "visit Mr. Morgan." We knew exactly what that meant.

Mr. Morgan was a friend of our parents who owned a nice little property outside of town that had a creek running through it. We would go there as a family sometime during the Fourth of July week and spend the day there. Almost always we would put a watermelon in the creek to let it get good and cold, and then my brother and I would "swim" in the creek. The water always felt delicious on those hot days! We would shimmy over the rocks and feel the white, grainy sand on our stomachs and laugh up a storm. Later on we would enjoy some fried chicken and potato salad together, and, when the time was right, we would fish the watermelon out of the creek and cut it.

There is truly nothing like a young boy eating a large hunk of watermelon with only his hands, letting the juice run down his chest as he devours the ripe redness and then spitting out the seeds like a Gatling gun. Oh, the glories of summer at Morgan's Creek!

Back at school, though, a day vacation to Morgan's Creek just couldn't hold up in the telling to other kids' descriptions of their week spent at places like Myrtle Beach. After getting tired and embarrassed explaining that we hadn't really gone anywhere outside of Williamston, Steve and I one day came upon a marvelous idea.

When other kids asked where we had gone on vacation, we determined to save face by doing a little "packaging" of our vacation concept. Rather than say we had only gone to the creek, we decided to tell the other kids we had gone to "Morgan's Beach." After all, there *was* white sand and we *did* get in the water.

I remember the first time we came back to school and someone asked me where we had gone on vacation. "We went to Morgan's Beach!" I told him.

"Where's that?" my friend asked.

"Oh, it's a really neat place!" I told him. "I can't really tell you how to get there because it is kind of hard to get to."

And that was the end of it. I discovered even at that early

age that most people really aren't interested in hearing anyone else's story. They mainly just want to tell their own.

The real truth hidden in my little heart was that I couldn't tell anybody else how to get to Morgan's Creek because I didn't really understand how to get there myself. I was too ashamed: ashamed of my mill hill upbringing, of my poor family, of making a poor showing in comparison to others' vacations, and ashamed that deep down, everyone else was better than me. My self-esteem would have fit in a thimble. At the time, I had no idea how precious or how wonderful my life was.

In the years since my childhood I have been privileged to visit beautiful beaches in many parts of the world. I've been to Myrtle Beach, Daytona Beach, Hunting Island, Waikiki, and the Arafura Sea. I've been to the world's two largest barrier reefs in Australia and Belize and have traveled to seashores too pretty to describe adequately.

Yet the days spent at Morgan's Creek are golden to me now as once again I see with my mind's eye that green watermelon rolling around in the cool water, and I hear my father and mother laughing at my brother and me as we run and splash each other in the creek. We were a family, and the days of "vacation" spent at Morgan's Creek were beyond price. I wish that the days had been weeks, for there was never enough time to spend together there. But there never is, is there?

I look back and wonder now how something so precious to me as our family being together, playing and laughing on those bright, sun-kissed July days could ever have been considered inferior to anyone else's dream vacations. They were, in reality, simply wonderful, and I would not trade those memories now for anything.

How many other priceless events in our lives do we pass over because we are looking around and expecting something better? How many hopes and dreams of our lives do we put aside because there might be something else better somewhere out there? Can it be that some of the most precious times of our lives are right here and right now, and yet we fail to see them because we have allowed ourselves to become dazzled by other things?

If you want to go there, I think I can tell you now how to get to Morgan's Creek. It is the place where our children play and scamper through our homes. It is the table where we as families enjoy a meal together and talk of the day's happenings. It is that place in our own backyard or anyplace else in the world where our little family talks and laughs and doesn't care whether the world passes us by or not.

You see, Morgan's Creek can be anywhere and anytime for us if we will just open our eyes and realize how incredibly blessed we are right now to have the privilege of being together with the family the good Lord has given us. The hope that we have for better days can be enjoyed even here and now if we will just exercise a little faith and understanding. And though the chances to go to Morgan's Creek seem to slip away from us as we age and our kids grow up, there is really nowhere else in the universe I would rather be.

May I invite you to go with me to Morgan's Creek? Better hurry, though. Daylight is wasting.

## 1.2
## Getting Across the Ditch

*I can do all things in him who strengthens me.*
— Philippians 4:13

"YOU JUST CAN'T GET THERE from here!"
How many times have we heard that? Sometimes that is the way life is. Have you ever, while trying to accomplish something that you considered important, run upon barriers that have threatened to stop you in your tracks? Most of us have. Worthwhile things don't come easy, do they? There is a price to be paid and a sacrifice to be made if we are to make a difference where we live.

What do we do, though, when the road that we must travel becomes really hard — so hard that we feel we can't go on? How do we forge onward when we can't even see a road ahead?

Several years ago I started out on a journey to meet with one of our leaders down in the coastal town of Malacatan in Guatemala. It was important for me to go see him. But first I had to make a stop in Tajumulco. It was just as well, I thought, because there was a back road from Tajumulco down to Malacatan, allowing me to get several things done in the same day. So I headed out from Ixchiguan to Tajumulco in our gray Toyota Land Cruiser.

After I finished meeting with the brothers in Tajumulco, I headed down a dirt track to the coast. It was a clear day and the sun was shining, making it a welcome contrast to the cold of Ixchiguan. As I drove, I wound around through little villages and watched the vegetation get greener and more tropical.

I continued on for about 45 minutes and was getting close to where the road ran back into the main road when suddenly I had to slam on the brakes to avoid a huge ditch that had been carved across the road! (No warning signs anywhere, of course!)

It turns out that the community was in the process of putting in a drainage ditch. On the left side of the ditch there were some trees, and on the right side was a drop-off. I couldn't believe it! The road was completely blocked with this six-foot ditch, and both sides were impassable. There was no way to go forward, no way to go around, and I was too far along on the road to just turn around and go back. It would have taken me another three hours to retrace the way that I had come and go down the mountain way. There just wasn't enough time to do all that and still get there in time. I absolutely had to meet with the brother in Malacatan. He was there already and waiting for me. Like it or not, I was committed to the road that I had chosen.

I got out and kicked a few rocks in the path to vent my frustration, and then wondered for the umpteenth time in my life why things have to be so hard! How was I supposed to go on when the road was blocked? What was I supposed to do?

Throughout our lives we are faced with obstacles and hardships to overcome. Some people seem to have more than their share. I have known many people who grew up in terrible homes. Some have suffered abuse. Others have endured alcoholic parents and dysfunctional situations that would stop an elephant. I have a close friend who lost his sight when he was 14. (Try losing your sight and see what that does to all your plans!)

Another friend felt called to be a pastor, but he had a stuttering problem that was so severe he could hardly talk. Other friends have felt called to mission service, but they couldn't see how to overcome all the roadblocks.

Growing up on the mill hill, I saw many people who were bright and intelligent but for whom an education wasn't possible because they lacked the money. So many barriers, and so much to be overcome for so many people.... Why does life have to be that way? What happens when we feel that we really can't get "there" from where we are?

Are the barriers in your life too much to face today? Do you ever feel that there is just too much to overcome to get where you know in your soul you need to be? If so, take heart!

The apostle Paul knew something about facing difficult barriers. In his early years (when he was known as Saul), his life had gone along so well! He had come from a good family, he was smart and capable, he had the best of educations, and he had risen far in his chosen profession. He even had the backing of some of the most powerful people in his country. He was a great success in the eyes of all who knew him! That was ... until he encountered something on the Damascus road that brought him to his knees.

Talk about a stopping point! When Paul got up, he was blind, confused, and it seemed that his whole life had been turned completely around. He could not go any further in his own strength. His way was blocked before him. He could not even see the road before him! He may not have known it then, but stopping at that "ditch" in the road that day would prove to be the best thing he ever did!

It was this same Paul who years later would pen what has become known as "the great love chapter" of I Corinthians 13, a collection of verses so beautiful and helpful that they have been repeated by Christians all over the world too many times to count! As Paul thought about life, he finally understood that there are some things that really matter and some that don't.

Three of the former things rose to the top of his list: faith, hope and love. Without these three things, no one can overcome the obstacles that must be faced in life. Without faith, we are lost without a compass and have no idea whatsoever which way we should go. Without hope, we have no reason to go on when our way is blocked and we lack the confidence to even try. And without love, there is nothing worth going on for, and the whole journey becomes a waste anyway. Faith, hope and love must abide in our lives if we are to keep going on. And, as Paul wrote, the greatest of these is love!

If we cling to our faith in Him, to our hope in Him, and to His love for us, we will find that no matter what barriers may lie ahead in the road, He will make a way for us. As the chorus says, "God will make a way/Where there seems to be no way/He works in ways we cannot see/God will make a way." He never told us that it would not be hard. After all, if it were easy … it would already be done, wouldn't it? But through faith, hope and love we can find the way to keep moving forward.

As I stood looking at the ditch in front of my Land Cruiser, I had no earthly idea what to do next. I asked the Lord to help me, and it was then that I remembered seeing some thick wooden boards drying in front of a house I had passed earlier. I drove back and, sure enough, the boards were about three inches thick and six or seven feet long. In my mind I measured the width of the ditch and thought about the weight of my car compared to the strength of those boards. To be honest, I had no assurance that the plan forming in my mind would work. But I did have faith in God, and I knew that He had inspired my plans for that day.

So I asked the family if they would rent me their boards for a few minutes. I got them into my Land Cruiser (most of the way in, anyway), along with a young boy from the family. I figured he had been sent either to help me or to make sure I didn't abscond with the lumber. Boy and boards — I hauled them all back to the big hole across the road. I got the boards out, lined them up with my wheels, and positioned them across the ditch, leaving (I hoped) just enough board on each side of the hole so that the edges would not collapse under my car's weight.

I lined up everything as best I could. Then came the moment of decision. It is one thing to think of what we should do, but it is altogether another thing to actually do it. I got into my car, started it up, and paused to consider once more the slim path the boards provided. If I slipped off, then I would probably ruin a $30,000 Land Cruiser, not to mention the effect it would have on my day! I asked the little boy to tell me if I started to steer off the boards.

Would you believe that the boards held, and that He saw me across that ditch, and that I made it to Malacatan in time to see the brother who was waiting for me? God once again had made a way for me. He is good at that!

What are the ditches that are stopping you from going God's way today? Oh, the holes are pretty deep, and the way can be pretty slippery — I know. But let me encourage you to open your eyes just as the apostle Paul did so long ago. See the way that God will open up for you if you will only depend on Him! He will always make a way for you and me as long as we travel the road He wants us to. As you travel down that road, have a little faith, a little hope — and mostly, a whole lot of love. Move on toward the goal of the high calling that He has set ahead for you. If you know that He is with you, then it does not matter how deep the ditches are for He will be there to see you through! And that is all that really matters.

May the impossible become possible through Jesus as we cross over the barriers that life puts before us. I'll even make you a deal. You watch the boards for me, and I will watch the boards for you. That way we both will get across the ditch. After all, there is a purpose for our travels, and a celebration up ahead awaits us.

Drive on!

# 1.3
## The Art of Worrying

*And which of you by being anxious*
*can add one cubit to his span of life?*
– Matthew 6:27

*Therefore do not be anxious about tomorrow,*
*for tomorrow will be anxious for itself.*
*Let the day's own trouble be sufficient for the day.*
– Matthew 6:34

T HE ANSWER IS "YES!"

At least, that is the answer given by the voice inside the head of the character played by Anthony Hopkins in the movie "Meet Joe Black." Only a little later in the movie do we find out that the question that Hopkins' character was struggling with was, "Am I going to die?" Yes, he was going to die and, yes, he did die at the end of the movie. His concern was a legitimate one indeed!

In another movie called "What Women Want," starring Mel Gibson, the character Gibson plays gets zapped by an electrical charge and suddenly begins to hear women's innermost thoughts. At first, he listens intently and is fascinated. Then he notices a pattern: the women around him worry all the time ... about almost everything! They worry about their looks, their weight, their relationships ... about their careers, their children

... about accidents, growing old and dying ... and about almost everything in between.

However, it is not only women who do the worrying. Although it is probably true that women worry more than most men, men worry too. So do teenagers and even children. The flat truth is that all of us worry about something from time to time. It's just that some of us worry a lot more than others.

Are you a great worrier? Yes, I see those hands! I understand — truly I do. You see, I too have been known to worry from time to time. Perhaps the more you live and experience, the more you have to worry about. At least that's the way it seems.

When we were children, we thought nothing about jumping off the roof of a building with only an umbrella in our hand. We assumed that we would fly just like they did in "Mary Poppins." Neither did we think twice about getting on any fast-spinning contraption at the fair. We just assumed that it would be safe and fun and that nothing would happen to us. It is only after we have lived enough to see a young girl nearly get her neck broken by a fair ride that we begin to wonder, "Is this thing really safe? I'm not so sure about it ... . What if that thing should malfunction while my child is on it!?"

The little guy from *Mad Magazine* known as Alfred E. Newman (with the chronic big, goofy, serene smile on his face) was famous for saying, "What? Me worry?" Apparently, he didn't worry about anything. And he was a complete idiot! Problems are all too real in this life, and facing them squarely will cause reasonable people to lose a little sleep every now and again.

Some of the questions that we all worry about are: Will my family be all right? Am I going to be okay? Is my work going as it should? Will my life count for what the Lord wants it to count for? Will I really have made a difference for good when my time is through? Am I going to get old and die after having faced a terrible illness?

If I were less honest, I would probably say we should just have more faith and claim more peace. However, I don't really believe that we can turn off all our worrying by just willing it to be so. We will always worry about something, more so at some times in our lives than at others.

However, the Bible tells us clearly that we cannot add one single extra day to our lives by worrying. We cannot stop earthquakes or tsunamis or lessen the wobble of the Earth by worrying. We can't stop illnesses or aging by worrying. Just the opposite, we probably bring on more problems such as heart illnesses (and worse ones too!) by worrying.

The Scriptures make clear that we should not worry about what might be tomorrow's problems because today's troubles are quite enough for us. Or, as our good friend Myrna used to say with a smile, "Don't borry [borrow] trouble!"

The Bible also mentions in Hebrews 2:15 that part of the reason Christ came into our world was to "deliver all those who through fear of death were subject to lifelong bondage." You see, while all of us worry from time to time, if we are not careful we will fall into a lifelong bondage to worry, and that is definitely not God's will for us! What He desires is that we learn to trust Him more and that we allow ourselves through that trust to be set free from the worst of our worries.

Finally, Luke 9:24 exhorts us that we would do well to "lose our lives" in Christ! There is a promise that those who lose their lives for Christ's sake will find life. In other words, we should be a lot more concerned with living out His will rather than hoping to control the circumstances of our lives and the lives of those we love. If we are rooted and grounded in Him as we should be, then no matter what may happen in our lives, it will be all right! He promises to grant us a good ending through Jesus Christ. And we can rely on that promise and trust Him to take care of us — even in all the things that we cannot take care of ourselves.

The answer is still "Yes!" Yes, sometimes bad things will happen in our world ... even to our loved ones and us. Yes, one day we all will grow old and die (if we are blessed to live long lives!). But, yes, He will be taking care of us as we trust Him and rely on His grace to see us through.

In the end, will it really be all right? The answer is always: "Yes!" And that is an answer that all of us who belong to Christ can live with, is it not?

So, go on! Worry a little, if you have to. But trust a lot! For He is trustworthy ... always, in all circumstances, and at all times!

And, no matter what, because of Him ... know that it is going to be all right.

## 1.4
## Battling the Black Dog

*For through the Spirit, by faith,*
*we wait for the hope of righteousness.*
– Galatians 5:5

*And let us not grow weary in well-doing,*
*for in due season we shall reap, if we do not lose heart.*
– Galatians 6:9

SOMETIMES IT SEEMS that you just can't win for losing. Over
the years we have known so many people who have struggled
with problems of all kinds, even as they tried to remain faithful
to the Lord. From time to time we too have struggled.

We hear almost every week from friends facing terrible
circumstances, including disease, troubled marriages, severe
financial crises, troubled children, doubt, work-related stresses
and many other heavy burdens. Some of us feel that we live in
an almost never-ending series of frustrations and setbacks that
leave us feeling almost as if life is too much to bear. If it is not
one thing, it is two. Have you ever felt that way?

Anyone who says that life is easy has yet to get out of his bed
in the morning! Life is hard — make no mistake about it.
However, admitting that life is hard is only half the story. The other
half has to do with how we cope when hard times come our way.

Once while serving as journeymen in the eastern jungles of Ecuador, we learned a valuable lesson that we find helpful to remember from time to time. As part of her work in Lago Agrio, Ecuador, my wife, Lily, trained groups of midwives who delivered babies in the remote parts of the jungle. Her purpose was to lower infant mortality by teaching simple techniques such as improving hygiene and boiling the instruments to prevent tetanus and other needless infections. In one of those groups, Lily taught several ladies who lived out in the middle of nowhere in an area called Wataracu.

From time to time, Lily paid visits to her ladies after the course to see how they were doing and how they were using what they had learned. On one of these visits, we drove the jeep as far as we could and then walked a jungle path for quite a way to get to where the midwife lived. I remember that it was a terribly hot day and the jungle growth was thick. As usual, we lugged Lily's heavy leather medical bag with us — just in case.

As we neared the little hut where the midwife lived, two dogs suddenly threatened us. They were black and bone thin with sharp, snarling teeth. They were not merely barking at us; they were set on attacking us. As was the custom with hunting dogs in the jungle, these dogs were not fed regularly. They ate only what they caught. On that day, it seemed that *we* were about to be their catch.

I stepped in front and began swinging the medical bag I was carrying at the dogs. One was on our right, the other on our left. When I swung the bag to the right, the dog on that side would step back a bit, but the dog on the left would take a step forward, and vice versa. My only hope was to keep swinging the bag back and forth in an arc that would keep both dogs at bay until we could figure something out. This went on for several minutes. As long as I could swing the bag, we were okay. The problem was that my arms were quickly tiring. I knew that if we did not get some help soon, we were doomed to be chewed up by two black dogs.

It is interesting to me that Winston Churchill used the image of a black dog to describe his depression, which he suffered from most of his adult life. He once said that the "black dog" was always around him, snapping at his heels, but that he was determined not to give in to it. To escape his black dog, Churchill turned his attention to addressing problems much bigger than his own.

He took on Adolf Hitler and focused his efforts on saving the free world by stopping the Nazis. When he devoted himself to fighting the big battles, he seemed to forget about his smaller ones for a while. He reached into his "leather bag" and pulled out hope, optimism, conviction in the ultimate victory of right over wrong — not to mention a bulldog determination to see the battle through to the end. It can easily be argued that were it not for Churchill's resilience in fighting the black dog of his depression, England would not have withstood the German assault of World War II.

What do we do when confronting the "black dogs" of our own struggles? Some people despair and give up. Others give in to helplessness and lose hope. Paul, in his letter to the Galatians, recognized that many battles were going on in the lives of the Christians there. He identified the "black dogs" that troubled that particular church and called them by name. Then from his bag of counsel he pulled out spiritual weapons such as waiting in the Spirit, having faith, living in hope, and not losing heart.

"And let us not grow weary in well doing," he advised the Galatians, "for in due season we shall reap, if we do not lose heart" (Gal. 6:9). These weapons are more than adequate in fighting back the black dogs of life.

In fact, because of those very weapons we won the battle with our two black dogs in the jungle that day. The Lord gave me power to keep on swinging just long enough until their master finally came and called them off. And so it is with many circumstances in our lives. If we do not give up or lose heart, the Master will step in and give us victory. No "black dog" can overcome us if, while we wait on the Lord, we simply use what He has already given us.

Faith, hope, patience, trust, endurance … these are mighty, powerful weapons to use when life seems too tough. All He expects of us is to use what He has provided and to hold on and not give in. In the end, He always shows up. In the end, He will see us through even the most trying of times.

No matter what you may be facing today, no matter what your "black dogs" may be, trust in the Lord and don't stop swinging until He tells you to.

## 1.5
## The Stuff Dreams Are Made Of

*And Jacob was left alone, and a man wrestled with him*
*until the breaking of the day.*
*. . .*
*Then he said, "Your name shall no more be called Jacob,*
*but Israel, for you have striven with God*
*and with men, and have prevailed."*
– Genesis 32:24, 28

*And behold, there arose a great storm on the sea,*
*so that the boat was being swamped by the waves … .*
*And he said to them, "Why are you afraid, O men of little faith?"*
*Then he rose and rebuked the winds and the sea;*
*and there was a great calm.*
– Matthew 8:24, 26

AT TIMES IT CAN BE QUITE DIFFICULT to see the blessings of God in life's circumstances.

We know that the Lord is with us if we belong to Him, but when we look around at any given time, sometimes we see only trouble. There are a great many battles to be fought, and life at times can just seem too difficult. We look around and see struggles. We see broken relationships. We see storms and large waves breaking over us. What we often don't see is the presence of God with us in these difficult times.

Life is tough. Relationships are tough. Have you been misunderstood or — worse yet — ignored lately? Have you tried to tackle one problem only to encounter two? Are you putting long hours into the battle with no end in sight? If so, you qualify to be part of the human race. Everyone experiences problems, communication breakdowns, struggles and misunderstandings. These are common to us all. It has always been so and is still so today.

We read in the Old Testament that Jacob had a very broken relationship with his brother Esau. You remember the story. Jacob had bartered Esau out of his birthright with a bowl of bean soup. Then the time came that he wanted to make things right with his brother. Jacob prepared his family and his servants to go before him in his best effort to mend a relationship that he cared very much about.

But before he could even get near his brother to patch things up, he had to fight an unexpected battle with a stranger. As the old saying goes, if it is not one thing, it is two. Out of nowhere appeared a man who proceeded to wrestle with Jacob throughout the night. It was a fight like he had never had before. He fought until his strength began slipping away, and, if that weren't enough, his hip was thrown out of joint. Weak, injured and weary, Jacob still would not give up. He hung on and refused to give up the battle, even as the dawn broke. In the end, his persistence paid off.

In the New Testament, the disciples of Jesus had their own problems. (Did you ever wonder where they got their food each day if none of them any longer had a paying job?) As they followed a man who insulted the power figures of both the church and government and who stayed just one step away from being stoned or pushed over a cliff, they truly lived life on the edge.

If that were not enough, as they sat together in that little boat on the Sea of Galilee one day, the storm grew so fierce that they just knew their lives were over. The wind howled, the waves swept over them, and they began to despair. Jesus was in the boat with them, but He was asleep! *Of all the times for Him to take a nap*, they must have wondered. Why couldn't He have slept when things were peaceful and they weren't one gulp of seawater away from death? Facing the storms was not easy, even for the disciples closest to Jesus.

How can it be that Jesus can be so close and yet life can be so hard? That is a question that has haunted God's servants through the ages. Popular Christian music and the regular fare of health-and-wealth preaching tell us that when we are near to Jesus, life gets peaceful and smooth. Our experience, however, tells us that this is just not the case! But why is it that there are so many storms and battles to be faced by those who are in the will of God? (Apart from the consequences of sin in our lives.) I think that part of the answer to that question relates to some intrinsic value of our persevering in those battles that are worthwhile. Another clue may be related to our perceptions of the battles and storms we face.

Jacob may have had a terrible night and a painful next day with his hip all out of joint following his long fight, but I wonder how he would have described it a year later? To have "striven with God and with men" and to "have prevailed ... ." How many can lay claim to that? All those hardships and that long night of wrestling with what he did not understand ultimately helped transform him into his new identity: Israel.

Because he did not give in to defeat, he became a mighty man of God who was used to carry out God's plan in settling His people in the promised land. What if he had given up and not fought on? I suspect that the future of Israel would have been altered. He might not have asked for or wanted the battle, but his persistence and endurance served its purpose. There truly is an intrinsic value in not giving up.

What about the disciples? Although the storm had scared them to death, how did they feel about it years later? I suspect that every one of them looked back on that time and boasted of how they had seen the Lord perform a miracle in their midst by calming the storm that had threatened their lives. What seemed like sure defeat and disaster when they were going through it turned out to be an opportunity for God to show His power in their lives and circumstances.

Perceptions of what we face vary greatly depending on whether we are presently enduring a trial or whether we have already made it through the storm. What may seem like God's falling asleep on us when we need Him most could turn out to be the greatest example of His moving in our lives that we will ever experience. It all depends on how we look at it.

Carly Simon once wrote a song, "The Stuff that Dreams Are Made Of," about our perceptions of life with all its struggles and even, at times, its boredom. Her point was that we don't always realize that what we most want out of life may be right there in our everyday experiences — right before our eyes, only we don't recognize it. Could it really be that the battles and storms of our lives are really, as Simon writes it, "... the stuff that dreams are made of ... the slow and steady fire" and our "heart and soul's desire"? Is it possible that the ordinary, day-to-day events of our lives hold the potential for defining our character and for revealing our strengths?

If we think about it, would we really want to live a life that had no struggles and no storms to contend with? I think most of us would prefer to experience and know God's power in our troubling circumstances. If we never fought, how could we ever win? If we never endured the storms, how could we appreciate the calm that comes afterward?

If you are tired of wrestling with foes through the long nights of your existence, or if the wind and the waves seem about to overtake you, know this: God is with us, especially in our struggles. Sometimes the battles lead to great victories. Sometimes the storms lead to our experiencing firsthand God's great power. At the end of the day, we will be glad to have fought — and won. We will be glad that we knew the fears of the storm and felt the saltwater sting our eyes only to witness His calm when our hope was almost gone.

If you are struggling today, hang in there. Though the battle may seem fierce and the storms mighty, deliverance will come. There is a sunrise coming to end your long night.

There is one who will rise up and put an end to the storm in our lives if we do not lose heart. And His name is Emmanuel … God With Us!

# CHAPTER TWO

## Facing Our Dark Side

## 2.1
## When the Wrong Doors Get Opened

*And your ears shall hear a word behind you, saying,*
*"This is the way, walk in it," when you turn to the right*
*or when you turn to the left.*
– Isaiah 30:21

---

*There is a way which seems right to a man*
*but its end is the way to death.*
– Proverbs 14:12

---

*... These have chosen their own ways .... [W]hen I called,*
*no one answered, when I spoke they did not listen;*
*but they did what was evil in my eyes,*
*and chose that in which I did not delight.*
– Isaiah 66:3–4

SOMETIMES WE HUMANS are such obstinate creatures! We are always ready to take off, aren't we? An idea comes into our heads, and we decide to go in that direction no matter what. When one door doesn't instantly open up to us, we insist on opening our own door. We forget to ask God if we're going through the right door. And even when we do ask, if we don't hear the answer we want fast enough, we assume that surely God would want us to be happy — get a big raise, move to a better place, do something more fun, etc. — and we go ahead and open the door that seems the most promising for our situation.

We decide that we want to go in a certain direction, and we just make it happen ... because we can. How many people (including those of us in ministry) have accepted jobs, gotten married, gotten divorced, changed churches or fields of service, or opened up some other door of possibility merely because we wanted to without really seeking whether or not it was truly the will of God? We seem to have a habit of fabricating our own justification for whatever we want to do.

I once saw an interview on "Larry King Live" with former President Bill Clinton. Larry asked the former President why he had engaged in so much sexual misconduct, including his involvement with Monica Lewinski while serving as President. Clinton's answer was interesting. He said, "I did it because I could." What an honest answer! Bill Clinton, along with multitudes of others, open doors in their lives to do what they want (regardless of whether those things are good or evil) basically because "they can." We all have the power to force open the doors in front of us so that we can go the way we want. But deciding what doors we want to open can often be a tricky business.

A few years ago, we had a work team come help us in Ixchiguan. One of the team members, Tom, was on his first trip to our area. We arrived late that first night after traveling many hours from the airport in Guatemala City all the way to our home in Ixchiguan.

As Tom was getting oriented that first night, we told him to make himself at home. Like several others on the team, Tom felt tired and dirty, and he wanted to take a shower before he went to bed. We explained to everyone that the towels were in the closet just in front of the bathroom, and everyone could help themselves. Tom talked and played cards with us while he waited his turn in the shower.

When Tom's turn finally came, he walked into the bathroom and turned on the water. It was a cold night, and the water was good and hot. He took his time and had a nice shower. As he finished, however, he realized that he had forgotten to get a towel. So he stepped out of the shower and, opening one of the nearby doors, started feeling around for a towel. The closet must be huge, he thought, as he reached further into the dark space. Naked and dripping wet, he still could not find a towel, so he took another step into the closet with his arms outstretched, continuing to feel around. Unfortunately, Tom wasn't in a closet, and there were no towels to be found there.

A couple on the team, Grady and Judy, had already gone to bed in their assigned room that night — which happened to be our master bedroom. As they drifted off, they heard the door that led from their room to the bathroom swing open. Grady looked up to see Tom, in all his nakedness, stepping into their room with his arms out, groping in front of him.

It was then that Grady asked Tom, "What in the world are you doing?" Tom, realizing his mistake, blushed like a beet, apologized profusely, and quickly shut himself back into the bathroom mumbling, "Oh no ... oh no!" As embarrassing as it was for Tom, it was hilarious for the rest of us!

There are times when we all are faced with the difficult decision about what doors to open. Some of the doors we open are right because we have listened to God's direction and are going where He wants us to.

At other times, we bullheadedly open the wrong doors just because we want to go that way. And sometimes we can't even

40

tell the difference. The problem is, every door we open either leads us away from the will of God or closer to where He wants us to be.

I am convinced that some of the biggest sins (and the messes made by those sins) start with the opening of just one door. Jealousy or anger opens the door to hate and leads ultimately to murder. One lustful thought opens the door for an affair. One homosexual encounter opens the door to being given over to a God-forsaken lifestyle. One hateful thought opens the door to an estrangement that can last a lifetime. One drink opens the door to alcoholism. One snort of cocaine opens the door to drug addiction. One cigarette leads to nicotine addiction. One decision made out of our unbridled pride and taking control of our own destinies opens the door to our being the "gods" of our own lives. (A case of the stupid leading the stupid?)

Think about it. Nearly every terrible condition of our lives started with our opening one little door ... . It is after going through one wrong door that we then are faced with going through another wrong door ... and another and another until we are led further and further from where God wants us.

On the other hand, some people resent it when God doesn't open the doors they wanted Him to. Do you ever resent that you did not get that pastorate or position you desired? Or maybe you were not promoted at work or recognized for your valuable contributions? Maybe you didn't marry the person you dreamed you would or have the children that you imagined. Ever wonder why God did not give you the gift that He gave someone else? Some people pray and pray for very specific things, and God's answer is "No!" Sometimes, as the old country song says, "Some of God's greatest gifts are unanswered prayers."

Sometimes we are not led to open certain doors because they are not right for us. They would not lead us to the will of God that He wants us to experience in all of its fullness. After all, God really does know better than we do what we need and when we need it.

Only a very foolish person thinks himself perfectly capable of deciding on his or her own which doors are best. Just going after whatever we think will make us the happiest at the moment is not the way to go. There truly is a way that seems right to a man, but the end of that way leads to death. Each decision changes things, and each decision bears its own consequences — consequences that we cannot escape.

Opening all our own doors without asking God for His will in each matter brings only frustration and unhappiness. It also takes us away from where we need to be in order to walk through the doors that God has planned for us, causing us to miss the best opportunities of our lives. I am convinced that at times we cannot receive the special things God has for us merely because in the past we chose to open doors outside His will … leaving unopened the doors that would have brought us fulfillment and contentment. We become like my friend Tom, naked and grasping in the darkness for something that doesn't even exist where we are looking. The wrong doors never lead to the right places.

My word of caution to all is that we need to be very careful in the decisions that we make, taking great care that we don't stubbornly insist on opening any doors that lead us in any direction that doesn't bring us closer to God's will. Although it is very hard to always get it right, daily prayer and meditation on God's Word are the keys to knowing down deep in our souls that we are walking only through those doors that God has for us.

In other words, if God doesn't open a certain door for you this week, don't walk through it! Ask Him and wait on Him for the direction and decisions of your life. Otherwise we are left just like Tom, wishing that we had not opened the wrong door!

## 2.2
## Things We Encounter Only in the Darkness

*... [T]he people became impatient on the way.*
*And the people spoke against God and against Moses.*
*"Why have you brought us out of Egypt to die in the wilderness?*
*For there is no food and no water,*
*and we loathe this worthless food."*
*Then the Lord sent fiery serpents among the people,*
*and they bit the people, so many people of Israel died.*
– Numbers 21:4b–6

WHY IS IT THAT WE are never satisfied? We, who have so much, always seem to expect more! Bigger, better, more gratifying, more fulfilling, more opulent, easier .... We seem to want God to constantly flood our lives with ever-increasing dazzle. For many of us, too much is never enough! No matter how many blessings God has given and no matter how much grace we have received in the past, our predominant reaction to our present is too often to shake our fists toward God and demand, "What have You done for me lately?"

In the case of the children of Israel, God had already done extraordinary things! He had heard their cry as they lived in slavery in the foreign land called Egypt. He had sent them a deliverer called Moses and had secured their freedom. As they fled captivity, God parted the Red Sea and held back the waters so they could cross. Not only did He see them safely through, but He also drowned the enemies pursuing them.

Then, as God began preparing them to inherit a new "promised land," He led them on a new part of their journey. He had already moved them away from all the external bondage that had enslaved them in Egypt. Now He directed them through an interim period in the desert to face their inner bondage.

This whole process — this journey to becoming more like Him — was hard! But through their difficulties in the desert of their lives, God helped them to grow. Step by step, He moved them closer to becoming the people He had always wanted them to be.

While the Israelites were in this "desert of becoming," God provided them each day with a miracle food known as "manna" (one possible meaning of which is "What is that?"), which sustained them. God also provided them with His presence as they endured each hardship of their journey. How much more could you possibly ask for?

All that God had given them in the past, however, was not enough! They wanted more ... a lot more — and fast! And so they rebelled against the Lord as they tried to make their way around the land of Edom. Their rebellion caused them to walk in the dark land we know as "I'd rather do things my way!" They had decided that God's ways were not good enough and so began to walk in darkness, where they encountered things they hadn't expected.

Many years ago when Lily and I were in college, we lived in a very nice apartment right across from Anderson College. It was a wonderful apartment! However, we were transferring to Clemson University and were hoping to move into some brand-new apartments there. Since we had a projected date for when our new apartment in Clemson would be ready, we gave our landlord a date when we would be out of our apartment in Anderson. But there were delays. ... And when the time came for a new couple to move into our apartment, the one in Clemson still wasn't finished. We were stuck with no place to call our own!

We were offered another little apartment in the basement underneath our old apartment until our promised place in Clemson was ready. As we moved into that little basement unit, we grumbled impatiently about why we couldn't just move into our new promised housing!

The light switch in the basement unit was located on the far side of the living room, which meant that you had to cross the room in darkness to turn on the light. As I made my way across the floor with an armload of things that first evening, something moved underneath my feet. Slightly panicked, I started kicking at the thing, stomping and stomping until I sensed it had stopped moving. My heart was racing as I finally reached the light switch and dispelled the darkness of the room. What I saw in the middle of that floor was, to my horror, a snake! It wasn't exactly what you would expect to find on your living room floor, but nevertheless, that is what we stumbled upon while walking in the darkness that day.

I have thought back upon this experience many times. Why was there a snake in a basement apartment? Short answer: I don't know. But I do know that if we hadn't been walking across our apartment in the darkness, we would have seen the thing and could have avoided it! It was because I was walking in the darkness that I stepped upon a snake on my living room rug!

I sometimes wonder how many dreadful things we avoid by walking in the light of Christ. At times we ponder the things we have given up in order to serve God, but too seldom do we ponder the heartbreaking paths that we have avoided because God has led us along His paths of light! How many things that slither in the darkness do we miss because we are able to walk on a lighted path? What kind of life-threatening and life-ruining experiences do we avoid each day as long as we walk in the light?

I don't really know, but I have a sneaking suspicion that there were snakes all over the place in the desert area of Edom where the Hebrews had been traveling. I wonder if the only reason that the Israelites had avoided them was because they had been walking in God's light and hadn't had to worry about things that slithered in the darkness. It was only when they began to leave the light to walk in the darkness of grumbling ingratitude that they encountered the snakes. Notice also that when they returned to obeying the Lord, He took care of their snake problem in a unique way!

Are our lives going well? If so, is it not because we are walking in God's light? If, however, we are walking along dark paths, are we surprised at the "serpents" we encounter? After all, when we walk in darkness, we tread upon things God never intended us to. Ego problems, family issues, adultery, work problems, addictions to greed, alcohol, drugs, sex or power ... these are just some of the "serpents" that we run into when we leave God's paths of light to walk in our own dark ways. The results of walking in darkness are always painful!

I suggest that if we can't find "God's light switch" before we walk into a room, that we simply don't go there! Without His light, we will stumble on the things that slither beneath our feet.

Let us be grateful this week for the light of Jesus Christ that allows us to walk in God's paths. And may we be thankful that through Him we can avoid the many terrors hiding in the darkness.

## 2.3
## Hope for Deliverance

*We know that the whole creation has been groaning*
*in travail together until now; and not only the creation,*
*but we ourselves, who have the first fruits of the Spirit,*
*groan inwardly as we wait for adoption as sons,*
*the redemption of our bodies. For in this hope we were saved.*
*Now hope that is seen is not hope. For who hopes for what he sees?*
– Romans 8:22–24

*When I was a child, I spoke like a child, I thought like a child,*
*I reasoned like a child; when I became a man,*
*I gave up childish ways.*
– 1 Corinthians 13:11

Have you ever taken inventory of your heart and been forced to admit to yourself that you don't like what you see? The selfishness, the scars, the stubbornness, the estrangement, so far from where God meant for it to be … . So many things that we wish we could change about ourselves!

Yet it is a rare thing to make profound and lasting changes in a human heart. How many good intentions to grow into Christ-likeness have turned out to be fruitless endeavors? It is so hard, this process of being transformed into the image of our Lord. Yet when we do occasionally see and feel a genuine change in our old heart, it is a wonderful thing!

Experiencing real change in becoming more like Christ is one of the things that makes life so grand. No one ever said it was easy, but through the power of the Spirit we can change some things about ourselves.

We don't have to remain selfish, narrow-minded, unloving or unkind. Our God is a God of second chances, and He gives understanding to those who humbly seek Him. Although it is very hard to change our sinful hearts and our set ways, through Jesus and the renewing power of the Spirit, we can be reborn and grow into someone new.

The question is: How much do we want to be transformed? Many of us Christians have become content with our present life and our state of being. Because we are saved, we feel we have accomplished the only major change necessary. Do we perhaps think that the rest of the journey to transformation is not worth the pain? Are we content with the state of our hearts? Or do we wish for Christ-likeness enough to allow Him to reshape us? Is that even possible in our situations? I have to believe that it is.

Years ago Paul Simon penned a song called "America" in which he talks about traveling across the country in search of meaning. At first he and his wife, Kathy, play games and laugh as they go along. They are excited to be on a trip. Then, as time passes, they become bored and complacent. Finally, as exhaustion falls upon them and she falls asleep while traveling on the bus, he comes face-to-face with his own heart:

> *"Kathy, I'm lost," I said,*
> *Though I knew she was sleeping.*
> *"I'm empty and aching and*
> *I don't know why."*

It may be that Simon's words also fit us sometimes in our journey in becoming. After we are first saved, we're excited and glad to be on a great trip! Changes come easily. We laugh and play games and are thrilled at the transformation in our hearts. But as time goes along, we often become bored and complacent, and we no longer are so amused with the process of changing. Finally, some of us become exhausted, too tired to make any more changes. It is in this state that taking inventory of our hearts is most difficult. If we are honest, some of us have felt like Paul Simon as we faced the silence, shocked at the state of our own hearts.

When we take a long look at ourselves, we realize how far short we still fall, and we have to admit to ourselves how much work there is still to do within us. It is not an easy realization, for honesty can be painful. Yet it can also drive us on in our quest for further transformation.

Several years ago a movie came out called "Regarding Henry." In it, an egotistical and manipulative New York lawyer (played by Harrison Ford) looks down on most people and treats them like dirt. He is wealthy, popular and much in demand. When he speaks, people listen. Because of his position, everything he does is right — in his own eyes. One day, however, he is caught up in a robbery and is shot in the head, leaving his brain damaged. When he awakens, he remembers neither who he is nor even how to walk or talk. He has to, in effect, start all over again.

At first, all view his circumstances as a calamity. Then, little by little, Henry comes to appreciate the wisdom of his physical therapist, who is not wealthy, powerful or well known but who lives happily and honorably. He is everything that Henry is not.

51

This causes Henry to see that there is much work to be done in his life and in his heart.

As time goes by, Henry starts his life over again, step by painful step. Slowly he transforms into a decent, caring person. He turns into a family man who loves his wife and his daughter and who expresses that clearly. He begins to treat others with respect and escapes his once all-powerful ego and his disdain for the opinions of others. In short, he becomes a caring human being who doesn't claim to know it all. Instead of being the authority on everything, Henry becomes a learner and a man who genuinely listens to others and cares about them. He begins to appreciate the journey of becoming and becomes more real and transparent. He is able to trade his heart of stone for a vulnerable and deeply loving one. If only we could do the same. ...

What kinds of changes do our souls long for today? If we could start all over, what changes within our hearts would the Lord desire us to make? Perhaps we would do well this week to take a long, hard look at our "heart condition" and honestly confront what we see. Do we need to become less selfish and more loving and giving? Do we need to turn our desire for being served into a desire to serve others? In the depths of our hearts, do we seek to make a greater difference in the lives of those around us? If so, there is hope for deliverance! Because desiring a new heart is the first step in acquiring one!

My quest and my great need right now is to experience firsthand more of the fruits of the Spirit. Galatians 5:22–23 tells us, "But the fruit of the Spirit is love, joy, peace, patience, kindness, goodness, faithfulness, gentleness, self-control ... ." I have in no way arrived in this regard, even though I have been on this road for more than 35 years. There is so much more that needs to be done in my heart and in my life! An abundance of these fruits is what my heart needs and what my heart desires! How about yours?

*Change my heart oh God,*
*make it ever true.*
*Change my heart oh God,*
*may I be like You.*

*You are the potter,*
*I am the clay.*
*Mold me and make me,*
*This is what I pray.*

– Eddie Espinosa

## 2.4
## A Higher Power

*... The Lord is the everlasting God, the Creator*
*of the ends of the earth. ... He gives power to the faint,*
*and to him who has no might he increases strength.*
– Isaiah 40:28–29

*But you shall receive power when the Holy Spirit*
*has come upon you; and you shall be my witnesses in Jerusalem*
*and in all Judea and Samaria and to the end of the earth.*
– Acts 1:8

POWER IS A MUCH SOUGHT-AFTER COMMODITY in our world today. Perhaps it doesn't get talked about a lot, but the desire for power is a driving force in almost every area of our lives. Oh, to be sure, most of us want power to control others in order to make the world a "better place." We only want power and control so that we can make others do what we think they should.

But things don't always turn out the way we plan. The grasp for power often splits boardrooms and businesses down the middle. Churches are divided. Relationships that were once built on mutual trust and cooperation are strained and weakened to the point of breaking. Power divides. It also corrupts. Power (or the desire for power) often turns us away from virtues such as humility, compassion, honesty and servanthood. Power is a dangerous drug — one that, if we aren't careful, will overtake us like Mr. Hyde took over Dr. Jekyll. In the search for power, we mortals tend to forget who we are and why we were sent into this world. Power, if we don't watch out, can overtake our common sense and become an addiction.

Although, by the grace of God, I am not an alcoholic, I have always had a great deal of respect for Alcoholics Anonymous. I know quite a few people who have been greatly helped by AA's Twelve Step program with its premise of relying on a "higher power" to help break the bonds of addiction.

Step One of this program calls on each struggler to recognize that "we are powerless over alcohol — that our lives have become unmanageable." The program then builds upon that foundation to seek help from outside oneself — to find help from "a higher power."

My good friend Grady and I once had an interesting encounter with a "higher power." In 1999 while we were working on the Mam Center in Ixchiguan, Guatemala, we had an overhead power line that we were desperately trying to get the power company to move. The walls of the structure were getting higher and higher, and still the power company had not arrived to move the lines. As we watched those walls climb closer and closer to the high-voltage line, we started to sweat.

I think it was actually my brilliant idea to get a tape measure and find out exactly how far the power line was above us. As we looked around for something to attach the tape measure to, all we could find was a long piece of steel rebar. We knew there was a danger in lifting a piece of steel toward the line, but we thought we could control it.

Yep, you guessed it. As we were measuring, the electricity apparently arced, and the rod bent toward the line. A blast of power shot down that bar and into our bodies. Even though I was wearing thick gloves, I felt the electricity enter my right hand and exit through a gash of about two inches that I had recently cut on my upper arm. Grady didn't have a gash. The power knocked him backward and blew a hole in his foot where it exited. It was miraculous that we were not killed on the spot! In fact, shortly after our incident, another man in our area was killed when he accidentally touched a power line that carried much less voltage.

Following our brush with one kind of higher power, Grady and I were definitely left powerless, and our situation had definitely become unmanageable! We had made contact with a higher power ... but obviously not the right one. Not just any higher power can help us fight our addictions.

As Christians, of course, we know who our Higher Power is. (And I am sure the founders of AA had no doubt, either.) We know where to search, but our problem is that we so often are willing to settle for a lower power: one that we can better control. The answer to our search for a higher power is none other than the Lord who, as Isaiah 40:28 says, is the "everlasting God, the Creator of the ends of the earth."

Our hope cannot be found in grasping for power from the sources that originate in this world. Our only hope is to confess, as Isaiah suggests, that we are faint and have little might of our own. Only by His power can we get things right. Forget about controlling others — gaining control of our own lives is hard enough! Only by bringing our lives in line with His will can we discover real strength and power.

Chapter 2 of Philippians says that our Lord Jesus did not try to hold onto His power and that equality with God was not something He grasped at. Instead, He emptied himself and took upon the form of a servant in order to accomplish the Father's perfect will. In verse 5, you and I are told to have this same mindset.

Herein lies a great truth: If we grasp for power, we will only end up making a mess of things and will fail. But if we can only empty ourselves of our vain ambitions and seek — above all else — whatever God wants, we will find that He gives to us more power than we can imagine.

Do you want to be a powerful person? Then become a servant. You see, true power comes only through the Holy Spirit. It is only offered to us so that we may become more effective servants of God. When this happens, we become His witnesses, beginning where we are and going to the ends of the Earth. Our God wants to empower us to break down slavery to sin and to bash down the very gates of hell in setting free those who are in bondage. If we were to really grasp this, all the ladder climbing and politics of power on this Earth would fall away as scales from our eyes, and we would see and understand that power is given to us only to accomplish His will and not to build our own kingdoms out of our own petty desires.

God's plan for the use of power is so much better. His plan leads to unity among those who truly seek His will, and it leads to the building up of the true kingdom of God. What would our lives and our world be like if we were to embrace this?

If today you find yourself feeling somewhat troubled concerning the issue of power in our world, why not join me in turning for help to a higher power? No, not to any source that originates from this world — especially not a high voltage power line! Let us forget the puny powers of our world that hurt, divide and destroy. Let us instead empty ourselves of lower ambitions and seek only to be filled with the higher ambition of giving ourselves over wholly as servants of the Living God.

It is my conviction that Jesus is to be our example in all ways ... even in modeling how to use power. With Him as our example, it's clear that too many of us have been following the wrong models that we have learned from this world. In doing so, we're like the inmate in prison who remarked to a fellow inmate as he was led to the electric chair, "More power to you!" If we seek whatever power we can from this world, then sooner or later we are bound to be fried! Earthly power is just not the way to go.

As in everything, isn't our supreme goal to be like Jesus? If any of us, driven by our desire to control and have our own way and to do what we think is best, is on the wrong road today, it is not too late to turn back. It is not too late to realize that an addiction to power can control and consume us and make us less than what God intended us to be. May you and I follow Jesus more closely, and may we learn to use the power that He gives us to become better servants. The power to serve. Now that is true power.

In this sense, I can think of only one thing to say from my heart: More power to you!

## 2.5
## Maintaining Genuine Faith
## in the Valley of Despair

*Now the eleven disciples went to Galilee,*
*to the mountain to which Jesus had directed them.*
*And when they saw him they worshiped him; but some doubted.*
– Matthew 28:16–17

*Now Thomas, one of the twelve called the Twin, was not with them*
*when Jesus came. So the other disciples told him,*
*"We have seen the Lord."*
*But he said to them, "Unless I see in his hands*
*the print of the nails, and place my finger in the mark of the nails,*
*and place my hand in his side, I will not believe."*
– John 20:24–25

*At night when evening shadows came a-creeping*
*and the sighing winds did blow ...*
– childhood song "The Jingaboo Man"

HAVE YOU EVER NOTICED that, after many of the mountaintop times in our lives, deep valleys soon follow? One day we are feeling so sure of our faith in God, and we are certain that we will stay on the straight and narrow. Then, the next thing we know, we, like the character Christian in *The Pilgrim's Progress*, somehow wander into the Slough of Despond. Many times after we have been on top of the world, we find dark moods, doubt and depression descending upon us.

59

How many pastors, after delivering one of the best sermons of their lives, have then stepped out of their pulpits only to find crises of faith awaiting? How many times have we heard that wonderful sermon and felt so stirred to faith, or have attended a Christian camp, revival or missions conference only to run straight into doubt as soon as we get back home? Oftentimes those who have gone on mission trips and have known the presence of God working through them in a wonderful way have returned to their homes only to find some of the worst battles of their lives awaiting them. For whatever reason, it seems to be a common experience that people of genuine faith find themselves caught up in battles of doubt and despair when they least expect it. Why is it that after mornings of sunshiny certainty there come evenings of creeping-shadow doubt?

## DOUBTING GOD'S PROCLAMATION

If you find that you can identify with what I have just described, then take heart — for you are not alone! The story of struggling with doubt is an old, old story. ...

Eve was the first person in our world to doubt. Adam quickly followed. They had the privilege of walking in the garden with God and talking to Him person to person. Yet they so quickly came to doubt the proclamation of God. He had given them the world on a platter, so to speak, while warning them of the consequences of disobedience. Yet they doubted that what He had told them was really true.

## DOUBTING GOD'S PROMISE

Abraham doubted God's promise. God had told Abraham that he would have a son with his wife Sarah. But as they grew older and more impatient, they doubted that what God had told them would really come to pass. Instead of waiting for God to deliver what He had promised, they decided to take matters into their own hands. Thus the birth of Ishmael by a slave girl ... and the beginning of the Palestinian problems that we are dealing with even today!

## DOUBTING GOD'S PROVISION

Moses doubted God's provision. When God told him to go and tell Pharaoh to let the Hebrew children go free, Moses doubted that it could happen. He didn't have the capacity to do it, he thought, and he doubted that God could provide what was needed in his life to fulfill His plan through him.

## DOUBTING GOD'S PRESENCE

Elijah doubted God's presence in the midst of his problems. Admittedly, Jezebel and Ahab were out to have him killed, and he had to run for his life. Remember his pitiful whimpering in 1 Kings: "I, even I only, am left." (Been there, done that!) The truth was that he wasn't the only prophet left. Neither was he alone with his doubts, for God was with him even when he didn't know it!

## DOUBTING GOD'S POWER

Peter doubted God's power. When Jesus was being held by the soldiers and awaiting crucifixion, Peter didn't see how any good could come from what was happening. He was more concerned with protecting his own skin. (In all fairness, at least he was there with Jesus through His arrest. Only he and John were anywhere near!) Peter just couldn't grasp how powerful his Lord truly was — more powerful than even death!

Thomas doubted the proof of Jesus' resurrection. He just couldn't believe it until he could touch the risen Christ with his own hands. Again, he was not alone. The disciples too doubted the report of the women on that resurrection morning. Some of them even doubted Jesus until He ascended to His Father (Matt. 28:16). They were just like us, weren't they?

Carlyle Marney, a brilliant but unusual Baptist preacher who served in North Carolina and Texas many years ago, was once hounded by a skeptical follower who asked him a string of questions to trap him into confessing his doubts. After a long series of questions about his faith, the young man shot, "And do you believe in the literal resurrection of Jesus Christ?" To which a weary Marney replied with a smile, "I do ... most days."

I think that what he was saying was that no one is perfect. No one lives without the dark shadows of doubt coming "a-creeping" from time to time. As it was for the anguished father in Mark, the cry "I believe! Help my unbelief!" could be the prayer of all of us, could it not?

God understands this. He knows us better than we know ourselves, and He loves us more than we love ourselves. He will never stop loving us or cast us away just because we do not have perfect faith! Instead, He allows us to reach out our hands and touch (if only we will) the scars that proved His faithful suffering to buy our pardon. If we, like Thomas, will keep looking at Jesus, we will see even our worst doubts turned into belief. He can and will handle any doubts that we might have if we let Him. After all, He really is the truth, the life and the way. He has absolutely nothing to hide, and our probing can only reveal more of His majesty, more of His glory, and more of His love. We will see this if we do not give up our journey and decide to make our permanent dwelling place in the swamp of doubt instead of climbing on up to the mountaintop of faith. Besides, what kind of dolt would stay bogged down in a swamp?

When you doubt, know this: Our salvation is not based on our having perfect faith in Him, but rather is based on His perfect faithfulness to us! We are saved by turning to Jesus and accepting His death on the cross to pay our sin debt and depending on His resurrection to set us free.

We must then commit ourselves and our lives to Him as our Lord and Savior and trust Him to do the rest. It is all by grace. We do not (and cannot) earn salvation — not even by having perfect faith. When we walk through the valley of the shadow of doubt, let us remember that we are the ones struggling, not God. He never fails ... so our salvation is secure in His hands. And it always will be. No matter what evening shadows may cross our paths, the sunshine of His gift of faith will always break through in the end.

You can count on it!

# CHAPTER THREE

## Trying to be Real
## (in a Pretentious World)

## 3.1
## Behind the Curtain

*Since we have such a hope, we are very bold, not like Moses,*
*who put a veil over his face so that the Israelites*
*might not see the end of the fading splendor.*

*…*

*… [B]ut when a man turns to the Lord the veil is removed.*
*Now the Lord is the Spirit, and where the Spirit of the Lord is,*
*there is freedom.*
– 2 Corinthians 3:12–13,16–17

I REMEMBER SEVERAL YEARS AGO skimming a book that asked, "Why am I so afraid to show you who I really am?" So many people spend much of their lives trying to be somebody else. Perhaps we fear that we're not good enough, smart enough, educated enough, interesting enough, or good-looking enough … on and on it goes.

Whatever our reasons, we become like Moses and veil who we really are, lest everyone see our true face and realize that the splendor we feel we should have is just not there.

Some of us feel that if everyone could see us as we really are, they would not respect or love us as much. They might view us as struggling. They might see us as weak and unsure. They might see us as the Lord sees us. And that scares us.

Do you remember the scene in "The Wizard of Oz" in which Dorothy and her friends listen, awestruck, to the Great Wizard until Toto starts growling at something hidden behind a little curtain in the corner? The dog chomps onto the curtain and pulls it back, revealing a little man talking into a microphone. How embarrassed the little man is! He tries to pull the curtain closed, but it is too late. Dorothy has already figured out that the Great Wizard is, in truth, nothing more than a tired, chubby, gray-haired man who for many years has hidden himself behind the curtain. His curtain gives him security, hides his defects, and causes others look up to and listen to him. Without his curtain and microphone, who will pay him any notice?

Then an interesting thing happens. Once Dorothy and her friends get over their anger at his deception, they start talking with the real person. He shares his story, admitting that he is searching for his way back home, just like everybody else. He becomes transparent with them and begins to relate to them as equals. And would you believe it? They find him a very colorful person in his own right. They like him! They like him even better as a tired, chubby, little gray-haired man than they did when he was the Great Wizard! Oh, there will always be some who prefer an image to a real person. But the characters who really matter in the story begin to know and appreciate him just as he is. And that is never just an ordinary occurrence.

Would I be too forward if I asked the question, "Who are we ... really?" If the truth were told, some of us would have to admit we don't yet even know. Others of us may have an idea of who we are, but we, like the Wizard, prefer to hide behind our own fabricated curtains. Perhaps we are missing the biggest piece of the puzzle of our lives. Perhaps also, by trying to play it safe, we are missing out on the incredible blessing of becoming whole.

What would happen if we took down our curtains and tried to be who we really are — before God and everybody? It might be interesting to find out. Being open, transparent and vulnerable is a risky proposition ... but it sure has its rewards.

There is so much that I do not know. But I do know that we don't have to go on wearing a veil or hiding behind a curtain to be loved and appreciated by God or anyone else worth knowing.

"Just as I am, without one plea ...." Remember those words? Maybe it's time to take down our veils and our curtains. Maybe it's time to just be who we are. Oh, some will not understand. Some will always prefer the hidden person to the revealed person. But that does not matter. What does matter is that the God who made us and knows us best also loves us most — just as we are! He knows that we are in the process of becoming. He is not through with us yet, and that is okay for now. We can take down our veils and begin to trust Him with who we are.

How about it? Which do you choose: to continue on like Moses with a veil over your face or to attempt to be the real you? Will God love you without your veil? Will others love and value you if your curtain is removed? Of course! You could go a lifetime trying to be some perfect person as so many people do. But maybe it's time for that second option — the option of letting down and just being who you really are, warts and all. That would be my recommendation. To me, real is better than plastic any day! As we walk in God's way, we don't have to pretend anymore.

In Christ there is freedom to be you and me. Paul said that God offers us a boldness to do exactly that! In Him we can just be real, and, as long as we are following Him, we can forget about trying to impress others. In the end, it's just not worth it.

It takes so much time and energy, and it really doesn't fool anyone — especially not God. So why not try being who you really are this week? Go ahead.

I see a little dog already beginning to pull your curtain back!

# 3.2
## The Snows of Santiaguito

... *"When you see a cloud rising in the west, you say at once,
'A shower is coming'; and so it happens.
And when you see the south wind blowing, you say
'There will be scorching heat'; and it happens. You hypocrites!
You know how to interpret the appearance of earth and sky;
but why do you not know how to interpret the present time?"*
– Luke 12:54–56

It WAS ACTUALLY COLD for the time of year in Guatemala. But it was nothing new. We hadn't been expecting any precipitation, but the sky was quite cloudy and gray. You could barely see the sky in Xela, even though it was 7:30 a.m. I walked out to the Land Cruiser to find it covered with a white, fine powder. I scraped some off the hood and looked at it. Then I cleaned off the windshield and mirror, and then cleaned off all the windows so that I could see out clearly. Better safe than sorry. ...

My thoughts wandered back to my younger days in South Carolina. It wasn't often that we got snow there, but when we did, cleaning ice and snow off windows was just as necessary as though we had lived in Detroit or Chicago. After all, you had to see to drive. ...

As I returned to my situation in Guatemala, I looked once again at the white power and smiled to myself. It really did look like a fine frosting of snow. But it wasn't. It was volcanic ash, which we were getting quite frequently as Santiaguito, the nearest active volcano, constantly spewed ash over us.

While looking at our faux snow, it occurred to me that things are often not as they appear. What other things fool us? The smile on someone's face that is not happiness but a mask covering their pain. The happy couple you had dinner with last week who is actually at the point of separating. The family with the nice car and house who are just one step away from bankruptcy. Often we can't know these things — or even guess them. No, things are not always as they seem, and sometimes we miss all the signs.

I once heard a story about a professor who was working late at his desk when one of his students came by. The young man had several questions about a famous sociologist of the late 19th century, Émile Durkheim, and the professor looked up from his paperwork long enough to answer his questions. After a few minutes, the student thanked him for his answers and left.

The next day when the professor arrived at the university, the campus was buzzing with talk about a suicide the evening before. When the professor inquired, he was distressed to learn that the young man who had thrown himself out of an upper-floor window had in fact been the same one who had stood before his desk asking questions about Émile Durkheim. Apparently, the young man had gone straight from the professor's office and killed himself. As the professor mulled over the boy's last conversation with him, he confessed to another colleague, "I know that he didn't come to me just to talk about Émile Durkheim a few minutes before he threw himself off a building! How could I have missed it?"

The sad truth is that we very often do miss it. Because we are too busy, too preoccupied, or too whatever, we often fail to see that others around us are in trouble and that they are calling out for someone to listen. We talk to them and tell them what's on our mind. We talk about our day, our problems, our plans.... But how many times do we leave without a clue as to the pain that a friend or even family member is going through? Probably more often than we would care to admit.

We are like the multitudes of people who followed Jesus and witnessed his ministry — and were still clueless. In the verses from Luke, Jesus remarks that while they are astute at interpreting some things, they totally miss the boat on others. We too have ample opportunities to see and hear and understand — but we just don't.

If you are hurting today, and no one seems to know or even care, I just want to say that I am sorry. I am sorry that we, the body of Christ in the world, often get so preoccupied with living our own lives that we cease to be available to help anyone else. It should not be that way. If your marriage is on the rocks, your children are in trouble, or your job or even your career is about to go down the tube, you need help, and you deserve compassion and care from the Christian community. If you look okay on the outside but on the inside are struggling with depression and don't know where to turn, you have every right to expect some understanding from your brothers and sisters in Christ. Forgive us for not being there when you needed us.

Some of us really want to be able to look and to really see — to listen and to really hear. We want to be more sensitive to the pain that so many people carry inside. And we want to do something to help ... even if it is just listening and caring.

Things are not always the way they seem, and we don't want to let a chance go by to be of help. Otherwise, we are as useless as the faux snows of Santiaguito.

*O Lord, please teach us to be able to interpret*
*the present times. There is so much that we miss!*
*Forgive our lack of caring and for not taking the time to notice*
*the signs that people around us give when they are hurting.*
*Open our ears and our hearts that we might*
*have understanding when someone is in pain.*
*Help us care enough to make time to listen,*
*to ask the right questions that invite sharing, and to scrap*
*our daily schedules if we can make a difference*
*in someone else's life. Help us to look beyond the way*
*things may seem and to search out the way things really are ...*
*and to really care about the difference. Because this is what*
*you call us to do as the body of Christ in this world.*
*It is in the name of Jesus that we pray.*
*Amen.*

# 3.3
## Coming Face to Face with How Much We Owe

*"A certain creditor had two debtors; one owed five hundred denarii, and the other fifty. When they could not pay, he forgave them both. Now which of them will love him more?"*
– Luke 7:41–42

---

*Now may the Lord show steadfast love and faithfulness to you! And I will do good to you because you have done this thing.*
– 2 Samuel 2:6

LET'S TALK ABOUT INDEBTEDNESS. How much do you owe?

No, I'm not talking about how much we owe on loans or bills (although many of us owe more than we should!). Let us talk about spiritual indebtedness. How much have others impacted our lives because of their service to the Lord and because of their investment in us?

From time to time it's good for us to be reminded of God's goodness to us through other people. I for one am indebted to a great many people who have blessed my life in so many different ways. I could never repay the many acts of kindness to my family and me. I can only remember all that has been given to me and be grateful.

Perhaps David had some of these thoughts as well when he expressed his deep gratitude to the men who had buried King

Saul on the battlefield (2 Sam. 2:6). David had been a loyal friend to Saul, even after Saul tried to kill him. After Saul's death, it was in David's heart to honor him with a proper burial; however, he was not able to get to Saul's body right away. In the end it was men from the tribe of Jabesh-Gilead who went out of their way and honored their king as best they could under the circumstances by burying him. David was grateful for their investment and never forgot their service to him. Their compassion touched David and reminded him of God's steadfast love and faithfulness.

As He did for David, God sometimes brings people from unexpected places into our lives to bless us and teach us something. Many such souls will never know the impact they have had upon my family. I still vividly remember one instance. ... It started when I walked into a Texaco office in the eastern jungle of Ecuador in 1981 the day after I had learned my father had died.

In those days, Texaco gave missionaries free rides on their "jungle plane" to and from the capital city of Quito. However, we could only fly on those days when the plane had empty seats. Many of our Texaco friends were paid huge salaries (one oil-driller friend of ours was making $1,000 per day), and Texaco's first priority, of course, was to get their employees where they needed to be when they needed to be there.

On the day that I walked into the little office, there was a long line of employees trying to argue their way into a seat. I took one look around and was quickly discouraged, certain that there was no hope of two missionaries hitching a ride. But if I were to have any hope of getting back for my father's funeral, I had to have that flight.

When I got up to the desk, I explained to the man in charge that my father had just died and that I was just hoping to be able to make it from the jungle into Quito. If I could just get to Quito, I could catch another flight to the States and make it home just in time for my father's funeral.

I will never forget the look in the man's eyes when he grabbed his pen.

As he scratched through one name, he asked, "How many seats do you want?"

"Two, if possible," I said.

He marked through a second name and said, "You got it … and I'm so sorry."

Texaco perhaps lost a great deal of money that day because it bumped two much-needed employees in order to help a poor missionary. Texaco also made a friend for life that day. In the many years since that time, wherever I am in the world, when I need gas and have a choice between Texaco and another gas station, I will almost always pull into Texaco. Now I know that my little bit of business is never going to make or break Texaco, but I still buy their products out of a heartfelt sense of gratitude to them. Texaco reminded me that compassion should always win out over regulations or profit. The business of helping our fellow man should always win out over any other kind of business that we may think is important at the time. And, most importantly, I will always remember, because of Texaco, how much a little grace and compassion can mean to people in need.

God invests heavily in you and me. He takes sinners like us, loves us, forgives us and cleans us up in our time of need. He leaves His imprint upon our hearts, and establishes a relationship with us that will never end. He also surrounds us with people whose servant hearts will bless, inspire and teach us. May we never forget all the benefits that God, through His people, gives us.

What investments have others made in our lives? Have we taken any time to thank those who have helped mold and shape us? Are we not better people and better servants of Christ because of their involvement with us? Perhaps today is a good day to remember and to love more deeply because of all that we have received from the Lord through those He has brought across our paths. Are you aware of your own spiritual indebtedness? If so, pass it on to others by touching and shaping their lives today.

Reach out and love others through Him in a way that they will never forget.

## 3.4
## The Blessings of a Liberal Soul

*A liberal man will be enriched,*
*and one who waters will himself be watered.*
– Proverbs 11:25

It was the late 1920s. Times were good for those involved in real estate in Detroit, and Bert Pascoe was one of those people. He made a good living for his family. They enjoyed living in a lovely home and driving nice cars (which few people had in those days). Bert liked to surprise his family every so often by buying a new car and coming home to take the family for a ride.

Although they were rich, they were not stingy with their money. Bert bought his meat from a local butcher and became friends with the man. From time to time, he found the opportunity to help the butcher, who was relatively poor, with problems that would come along. Their friendship deepened.

When the Depression hit, the Pascoes were hit hard. The real estate market sank to rock bottom, and Bert was left penniless. He lost his fancy new automobiles and would soon lose his home. There was no money to be had. Then he received a visit from his friend the butcher. The man, in spite of the Depression, was still in business. He came to Bert with an unusual proposition. He told Bert that he needed someone to deliver the meat to his customers' homes.

"I can't pay you much, Bert," he said, "but you could take home some of the meat that doesn't sell, and you could keep the truck at your house."

So Bert, the wealthy real estate tycoon who was my wife's grandfather, became Bert the delivery man for the butcher. This opportunity saved his home, put food on his table, and allowed him to keep working while others in similar situations committed suicide. Because he had been kind and helpful to others in need, Bert was taken care of when the tables were turned. My wife's mother, Lucy Pascoe, remembered how that act of kindness kept their family from going under during the height of the Depression.

So many times in our work with the Tajumulco Mam, a Mayan people who live in the highlands of western Guatemala, we have heard people say, "May God multiply the kindness many times over that you have shown to me and bring it back to you!" It has always been our experience that, just as we are given the opportunity to help others, God has always taken care of us and richly blessed us in our times of need through His people. We have always found God's provision for us to be more than ample. As the Scripture from Proverbs says, He has indeed enriched our souls and watered our lives through rich blessings.

*God, may we always be liberal in our love, our kindness,*
*and in giving of ourselves to others. And may we always*
*be "watered" by the results of a life lived in obedience to You.*
*We are blessed!*
*Amen.*

## 3.5
## What If?
✥

*"Blessed are those who hunger and thirst for righteousness,*
*for they shall be satisfied."*
...
*"You are the salt of the earth; but if that salt has lost its taste,*
*how shall its saltness be restored?"*
– Matthew 5:6, 13a

SOMETIMES WE JUST NEED to look at a matter from a different
viewpoint to find wisdom.

Have you ever tried to solve a problem by looking at it the
same way over and over without success, until, after a break or
a little time away doing something different, you were able to
successfully approach the problem from a different angle?
Sometimes when we tackle a matter from a new perspective, the
answer suddenly becomes very clear. A different view can
sometimes lead us to new discoveries about our world and our
purpose in it.

This doesn't happen very often, though. We each tend to get
so caught up in our daily grind that we become creatures of
habit rather than searching each day for a way to live our lives
so that we change the world.

Bobby Kennedy once had this to say about his brother John:
"Most people look at the world and ask, 'Why?' My brother

looks at it and asks, 'Why not?'" In the case of John F. Kennedy, this perspective worked very well. For others of us, though, tinkering with reality can get us into trouble. Indeed, attempting to look at the world differently can get us labeled as "dreamers." If we are not careful, we tend to become objects of ridicule by those who insist, "Why can't they just leave well enough alone?"

My wife, Lily, and I caught part of a strange movie one time as we were flipping through TV channels. In this movie, a monk was questioning God about why the bubonic plague had taken over most of Europe and had killed so many people. He was very angry at God and blamed Him for not doing something about it since He was supposed to be in control. To his great surprise, God replied that he, the monk who had the skills and knowledge to fight the disease, *was* His plan to do something about the plague! Because the monk had wasted his time blaming God instead of working on a cure, mankind would suffer its consequences for another 500 years! It was the monk, not God, who had failed. Hmm ... .

Why is the world so sick and so far off course from what it should be? How have sin and evil been allowed to grow to the extent that they are deeply rooted throughout the world? How is it that so many have succumbed to evil? How can students bring weapons to school and slaughter their teachers and classmates? What about terrorism, egotism, torture, self-righteousness, beheadings, nuclear-equipped tyrants, civil wars, and the breakdown of law and order? How can our world, with so many Christians living in it and praying every day, be so evil? Some who favor simple answers like to say that we should not worry, that everything is going according to plan.

Forgive me, but I don't think so! In fact, I think just the opposite is true — that the world is totally out of control and that things are going from bad to worse. I think evil is growing, and we are running with it as the demonic pigs did in Jesus' day — heading straight over the cliff! Even worse, it seems to me that it is getting harder and harder to tell the Christians from the bad guys. And that really disturbs me!

I have a few "what if" questions for us. What if the divine plan for overcoming evil and for growing God's kingdom against the darkness is in fact failing because *we* are botching it? In other words, what if we Christians are actually assisting the growth of darkness in the world simply by doing little or nothing to bring in God's light? What if the world has lost its flavor because we have ceased to be salt? What if, instead of blaming God for all the terrible things happening in our world, we stopped for a moment and realized that the blame belongs with us?

What if the things you and I do really matter — much more than we think they do? What if you and I are literally called to change the world, but we can only do so by being obedient in ways both small and large? Could it be that we have the power in our hands to combat the darkness and to bring in the light of God by simply staying close to Him and letting Him have His way through us each day? Has God placed in our hands the power to change the outcomes of not only people's lives, but societies and global challenges as well? Could it be that the picture of God's will is a whole lot bigger than we ever realized?

I have come to believe that we as ordinary Christians can literally change the world! By abstaining from personal sin and staying close to God, we can allow His power to accomplish unimaginable things through our lives.

The opposite is also true. So many examples of this come to mind. What if the man who led the revival in a little country church so long ago had had an affair with his pianist ... instead of preaching his heart out the night that Billy Graham came forward and laid his life on God's altar? What if the Allied soldiers who stood up against Hitler in WWII had let their prejudice take over and sided with Hitler rather than fighting against him? What if the original framers of the U.S. Constitution had given in to fears of what the human conscience might be capable of and had not written freedom of speech and religion into the Constitution? What if a man named William Carey had given up when he went to take the gospel to India and had quit during the first seven years that he saw no fruit for his labors?

What if the one who led you to the Lord had compromised with sin and given up before he or she led you to salvation? And what if you compromise or give up instead of staying faithful to God in your life day after day, year after year? What good will be left undone and what evil will have grown in its place if your salt loses its flavor?

The Bible says that those who hunger and thirst for righteousness are blessed and shall be satisfied. Oh, the difference you and I and a billion other Christians could make in this old world were we but faithful in the little things! Oh, the people we could influence were we but just a little more "salt" in our flavoring of the circumstances of others' lives over which we have so much influence!

What if we all drew closer to God and allowed Him to have dominion over us in even the smallest areas of our lives? Until we get to heaven, we may never know how many things in our world would have been different had we been more faithful in our walk with Him ... or how many things would improve even now if we drew nearer to God. Could it really be that world peace, global warming, the elimination of poverty, and the ending of so much human suffering lie within our hands? It is mind boggling, isn't it? I don't really understand it all, either ... but I suspect that our obedience to Him in even the smallest things matters — a lot!

Hey, anybody out there got any ideas brewing about how to win others to the Lord, inspire someone to find a cure for cancer or AIDS, prevent congenital birth defects, discourage teens from experimenting with sex or drugs, live out the gospel in such a way that everyone with any sense would want to embrace it, prevent people from using violence to play out their aggressions, or stop the next "bubonic plague" before it even starts?

What if it is you whom God is counting on to bring about these changes? Just thought I would ask.

CHAPTER FOUR

Coping with the Pain of Living

## 4.1
## The Christmas Buzzard

*For we do not want you to be ignorant, brethren,*
*of the affliction we experienced in Asia; for we were so utterly,*
*unbearably crushed that we despaired of life itself.*
*… [H]e delivered us from so deadly a peril, and he will deliver us;*
*on him we have set our hope that he will deliver us again.*
– 2 Corinthians 1:8, 10

THE CHRISTMAS SEASON is a time for the heart! For many of us, it is a time of great joy, peace and comfort. It's a time of celebration and recognition that Jesus Christ, the Son of God, was born into our world to one day give His life so that we might be saved.

When we think of Christmas, happy images come to mind. Remembrances of Christmases past, of all the family being together, and of the simple joys that the season brings fill us with laughter and satisfaction.

It's not that way for everybody. For some, the season brings much anxiety and stress. I don't mean merely the Scrooges among us who don't want to spend any money. I mean those who, for various reasons, become severely depressed and even suicidal at Christmastime. Some have lost loved ones and haven't recovered from the pain. For others, the loss of significant relationships (a boyfriend, girlfriend, marital separation, etc.) is causing great emotional pain. Diseases such as Alzheimer's, Parkinson's, cancer, leukemia and diabetes rob life of its joy and peace. Aging parents, troubled children, financial woes, loss of jobs … the list of stressors goes on and on.

I once read an article that called the Christmas season the "deadliest days of the year." The article stated that there are more deaths during these holidays than on any other. Heart attacks skyrocket. Suicides and attempted suicides rise dramatically. People are killed by family members and close friends. For folks in this category, Christmas is not something to look forward to; it is something to dread.

I once counseled a young man who had just attempted suicide. I asked him to please try to explain to me how he had felt before trying to take his own life. He told me about several relationships in his life that had gone sour. Then he described falling into a dark hole that he could not find his way out of. "I just kept sinking deeper and deeper," he said, "and it kept getting darker and darker until I had no hope left of ever getting out again." For him, suicide seemed the only way to end the pain.

One time we had a youth Bible study in our home. Although most of the kids seemed outwardly happy, toward the end of the meeting someone brought up the topic of suicide. One person wanted to know if you "automatically went to hell" if you killed yourself. A couple of people talked about extreme loneliness and isolation. Others described terrible family problems. It was shocking to realize how close to the edge some of these kids were … and nobody would have guessed it! Perhaps today you or someone you love is close to that edge and almost no one suspects it.

During the Christmas season of 1980, Lily and I took some time off from our work in the eastern jungle of Ecuador and headed west to the coast. From there we planned to drive all the way down the coast to Guayaquil and then take a bus down to Peru. As we drove along the arid coast, we traveled through many small towns that looked as if they weren't doing very well. The land was partly desert, and many of the houses were just ramshackle dwellings that were barely standing.

One house in particular caught our attention. It was a little wooden house with dried, unpainted planks and an old wood-slat roof. Perched on top were three buzzards! Lily and I looked at each other and said, "Whoa! It looks like that poor family is not doing well at all!" Nope, it is definitely not a good sign when you have three buzzards perched on your roof waiting ... just waiting ... .

Somewhere along the way that Christmas, we purchased some little Ecuadorian Christmas ornaments made by hand out of straw. We bought a little man and a little woman to hang on our tree, along with some angels and some other pretty things.

After we had picked out these ornaments, we came across what was supposed to be a little dove. However, we both thought that it looked more like a buzzard than a dove. So we bought it, and we've hung it on our tree every Christmas since. We do so because, although many years have passed, we continue to remember that little forlorn house with the buzzards perched atop it. Yet we refuse to give in to the despair and hopelessness that those buzzards represent. Hope is a choice for each of us, and we cling to it regardless of life's circumstances. No matter how troubled our lives may become at any given time, because Christ came into our world, there is always hope!

The apostle Paul talked in his letters to the Corinthians about terrible times in his life when he was so "utterly, unbearably crushed" that he despaired of life itself (2 Cor. 1:8). Sometimes he was threatened physically. At others he was spiritually and emotionally drained. His best friends let him down. He felt forgotten and even abandoned.

Paul was a real person, just like us, who suffered and who knew what it was like to experience pain, doubt and worry. When you and I think of Paul today, we usually think of him as a tower of strength! Yet he knew what it was to be discouraged, depressed and crushed. Paul could have focused on his troubles. Instead, he focused on his hope. "… We have set our hope that he will deliver us again," he said.

Are you experiencing difficulties? Does it seem like the hole you're in is getting deeper and darker? Does your hope seem to be running thin? If so, there is good news to be embraced. God is with us! He will never leave nor forsake us — no matter how many buzzards seem to be circling our rooftops.

The same God who has seen you and me through so many trials and problems is still there today to see us through again! He is the rock of our hope, and no matter how many "buzzards" are perched on our roof, He will be there to help us turn our buzzards of despair back into doves of hope and peace.

Embrace hope in Jesus Christ, and put your faith in Him today. And while you're doing that, put your arms around someone else who is hurting and remind him or her of the never-ending love of God. Shoo away the buzzards of despair from their roof and point them toward the dove of peace, which can only be found in Jesus.

Christmas buzzard ornaments may not be to everyone's taste, but I am sure glad that we have one on our tree to remind us that, in the end, His hope always wins out over our despair!

Hold onto hope through our Lord in every season of your life. He will be holding onto you!

## 4.2
## What Not To Do When Bad Things Happen

*As he passed by, he saw a man blind from his birth.*
*And his disciples asked him, "Rabbi, who sinned, this man*
*or his parents, that he was born blind?" Jesus answered,*
*"It was not that this man sinned, or his parents,*
*but that the works of God might be manifested in him.*
*We must work the works of him who sent me while it is day;*
*night comes, when no one can work."*
– John 9:1–4

THE PROBLEM OF HOW TO RECONCILE our faith to the bad that happens has been around for a long, long time. Indeed, it's as old as the fall of Lucifer from heaven.

How do we respond to tragic events that occur in our world? How do we account for evil, especially as it affects our loved ones and circumstances in our own lives? How do we deal with the problem of natural evil? It is not easy.

Many Christians struggle to explain the "why" of events such as the huge tsunami that devastated parts of Asia in 2004. "Why did this tragedy happen?" some asked. "What caused it? Was it the sin of those people or of someone else?"

Through the years I have read some Christians' attempts to answer these questions, and many of their conclusions have deeply disturbed me.

Following the tsunami, some prominent Christians hinted that it hit the South Pacific because God was punishing the people there for persecuting Christians. This answer troubles me a great deal! In the first place, who among us can know for sure that God was behind those deaths and that He willed it to happen? It is a frightening thing, to me, to try to attribute acts that we consider "bad" to the direct will of God. (There is a great difference in the minds of many of us who see a separation of the direct will of God from the permissive will of God; i.e., everything that God wills will be accomplished when all is said and done, but not everything that happens today is necessarily His will!)

Although the Old Testament records that God did sometimes use natural disasters for His purposes, it seems a foolhardy thing to say that all natural disasters occur because of the particular sin of a people and to draw the conclusion that somehow "they had it coming!" To follow this pattern of logic would put us on par with primitive cultures whose people offered a sacrifice to the soon-to-erupt volcano in order to appease the mountain gods. This, of course, is rubbish! I am not at all sure that we want to take this route and join the animists of our world! For that matter, if God always dealt swiftly in punishing miserable sinners, you and I would have been the first ones to get washed away, would we not?!

Job's friends addressed the problem of his illness and loss by asking what terrible sin he had committed to receive the suffering that had come upon him. As it turned out, Job was not being punished. He was never given the full answer for why things had to be that way. He was simply called to remain faithful to God — no matter what!

Sometimes circumstances we consider terrible produce good in the end. There is an old Russian story about a farmer who once had a handsome stallion. He delighted in his beautiful horse until one day when it broke loose and ran away. One of his servants ran to him and exclaimed, "O sir, what a terrible thing has befallen you! Your stallion has run away!"

The wise old farmer replied, "Perhaps ... but it is too early to tell."

The next day the stallion returned with another stallion even more beautiful than himself.

The servant rushed up to his master and exclaimed, "O sir, what a wonderful thing has befallen you! Now you have two great stallions instead of one!"

The wise old farmer just looked at him and said, "Perhaps ... but it is too early to tell."

Sure enough, the next day the farmer's only son was out trying to break in the new stallion when he fell and shattered his right arm, leaving it useless.

The servant came running up and cried, "O sir, what a terrible thing. Your only son is now crippled!"

But the farmer replied as before: "Perhaps ... but it is too early to tell."

Several weeks later a band of Russian soldiers approached the farm seeking new recruits to send to the front lines of battle — almost certainly a suicide mission. When they saw the son's crippled right arm, they passed him by.

The servant, beginning to understand the farmer's thinking, ran up to him with a knowing smile on his face and said, "O sir, you were so right. Your son's breaking his arm turned out to be a wonderful thing indeed!"

To which the wise old farmer only replied once more, "Perhaps, but it is still too early to tell ... ."

Perhaps we, like the wise old farmer, would do well to reserve judgment until we fully understand the big picture.

Can any good come of such a terrible tragedy as the Asian tsunami? As some have pointed out, there are more people dying without Jesus every month in the affected countries than the total killed by the tsunami. Although the deaths of so many are terrible, tragic, and impossible to comprehend, the help that the survivors received and the attention of Christians from around the world who are sharing the gospel in these countries is a very good thing. It is, in a sense, too early to see the "big picture" of this tragedy. This in no way diminishes the question "Why?" Nor does it do away with the tragic loss of so many lives. What it does do is offer the hope that good can be brought out of even the worst tragedies.

In his book *When Bad Things Happen to Good People*, Harold Kushner discusses the problem of what we consider to be "bad things" in the lives of ordinary people. (Of course, none of us can really claim the title of being "good." That fits God and God alone!) Kushner himself knew the agony of questioning why. His son suffered from a terrible disease that took his young life.

In exploring the different possibilities of why evil happens in life, he asks some interesting questions: Could it be that the event we see as bad is not really bad? Do bad things happen because God is not really good all the time? Does it have to do with God not willing good for us? Does this happen because God is either limited or because He has become self-limited in responding to natural evil?

Jesus' disciples struggled with some of these same questions: "Rabbi, who sinned, this man or his parents, that he was born blind?" Jesus told them that it was neither. Problems like these cannot be described or understood so simply. Jesus went on to say that even though this man was born blind, the works of God could be manifested in him! It was not a time for pointing the finger and assigning blame. Was this man a sinner? Of course! Was his sin the reason for his suffering? Apparently not. This was not a time for blaming or for trying to know the unknowable. It was a time for helping ... and that is precisely what Jesus did!

Perhaps there is no way to easily explain many of the bad things we see happening in our world. I think that events relating to human sin that bring tragic results are much easier to understand. Where man is concerned, disobeying God's direction always results in suffering. However, understanding earthquakes, tsunamis, diseases that run rampant, and other forms of natural evil are much more difficult. Each of us has to struggle with these issues. Who among us would dare to even pretend to have all the answers?

Aside from saying that our whole world suffers from the consequences of being a fallen world groaning for deliverance following man's choice to sin (Rom. 7:22), I am sure I don't have all the answers tied up in a neat little bundle to offer anyone. I do believe, though, that God is always good, that bad things are often just that, and that although God is certainly able to stop things that cause much pain and suffering, He in His divine wisdom sometimes chooses to allow them. And I still believe that in any tragedy the works of God can be manifested through the obedient, helping hands of Jesus' followers.

Wherever there is heartache and suffering, I believe that God is there — that He grieves for His children and that He is at work for good in even the most troubled situations. Our role always is to help in the best way that we can ... just like Jesus taught us!

It is not our role, however, to assign blame and to act as though we are God, pronouncing judgment upon those who suffer! God is the only one qualified to judge; He does not need us to do that for Him! He calls us to respond, not with judgment but with love and with compassion, and to help in any way we can. The rest must be left up to God. ...

## 4.3
## The Promise of His Presence

*"... [A]nd lo, I am with you always, to the close of the age."*
– Matthew 28:20b

I COME FROM A LONG LINE of hunters and fishermen. In his younger life, my father, Homer, was an avid hunter. So was my mother's father, Dan. Dad had some prize guns that he dearly cherished, and one day he decided to lend Dan his favorite gun because Dan appreciated that fine rifle just as much as he did. The deal was that my grandfather would use the gun as long as his health held up and then return it to my father.

"I promise you," he told my father, "that I will get your gun back to you before I die. You have my word!"

Years went by, and both my grandfather's and my father's health began to fail. It finally got so that my grandfather could no longer go hunting. One day there was a knock on the door, and my grandfather came in bearing my father's rifle. They looked at each other for a long moment. Then my grandfather put the gun in my father's hands and said with a smile, "Homer, I'm as good as my word. Here's your gun." A lifetime of promise was kept. His word was good.

When Jesus suffered the tortures of the cross, He was forsaken by most of His disciples and by His friends. He was given over into the hands of people who hated and despised him. On the cross, even his Heavenly Father turned His back on Him, causing Him to cry out, "My God, My God, why have you forsaken me?"

At the end, Jesus was utterly alone. He died alone so that you and I would have to neither live nor die alone. Jesus was the only one who was ever truly alone, cut off even from God in those last moments on the cross. But He who knows with His whole heart what it is to be absolutely alone promised it would never happen to us because He would always be with us.

Jesus' word is good! His word never fails, and you can know with assurance that He will bring to pass everything that He promised us. He said He would be with us as we seek to do His will. Always. Everywhere. In any situation. He said, "I will be with you." And He is as good as His word.

Feeling lonely as you tackle the work God has given you? Do the isolation and difficulty of the job wear on you? Did you perhaps remember the work He assigned you today but have forgotten the promise that goes along with it? Know this: We are not alone! The way may be hard, and we may feel lonely and isolated at times, but in truth, we are not alone — not ever. Because of His presence, none of us needs to bear the burden or try to do the work alone. He is with us.

We have His word on it!

## 4.4
## When Hoping is Hard

*Just as day was breaking, Jesus stood on the beach;*
*yet the disciples did not know that it was Jesus.*
*Jesus said to them, "Children, have you any fish?"*
*They answered him, "No."*
*He said to them, "Cast the net on the right side of the boat,*
*and you will find some." ...*
*That disciple whom Jesus loved said to Peter, "It is the Lord!"*
*When Simon Peter heard that it was the Lord,*
*he put on his clothes, for he was stripped for work,*
*and sprang into the sea.*
– John 21:4–6a, 7

*Jesus said to them, "Come and have breakfast."*
– John 21:12a

Easter is a holiday celebrated all over the world. For many, it is a time for parades, Easter eggs, new clothes and chocolate rabbits. For others, it is a remembrance of the death and resurrection of our Lord. For most of us in North America, I suspect it is a combination of both — a happy time full of traditions and celebrations.

Have you ever wondered why Easter is celebrated on different dates each year? It's because Easter is set for the first Sunday after the first full moon occurring on or after March 21.

Did you know that? How many of us ever notice the full moon each month? Unlike others in simpler places and times, many of us seldom take time to notice things like full moons, sunsets or sunrises. Maybe we should.

The wonders of the nighttime sky escape the notice of most of us today. But the ancients used to stare up at the sky and notice the movements of the sun by day and the moon and the stars by night. They followed the glory of the heavens and knew when planets, comets and asteroids came into sight. Before television, the nightly show in the sky was the hottest act in town. Now, weeks and months (even years?) go by without our even noticing. We stay inside, watch television until late, and then sleep in our square bedrooms on our soft queen- or king-sized beds.

The ability to sleep well at night is a great gift. Not everyone is so blessed. We have some friends who are kept awake because of different problems. One is unable to sleep because of muscle jerks that wake him every time he drifts off. Another friend has insomnia because of the trauma that he has suffered in his life. When he does sleep, he has terrible dreams in which he relives past horrors. Several others suffer physical pain that hinders their sleep. Have you ever noticed how much stronger pain is at night? For them, in the quiet of the night, pain becomes much more noticeable, and they struggle through the darkness awaiting the coming of the day.

Some in our world suffer at night from causes of which most of us are unaware. In the war-torn places of our world, people lie down and try to sleep without peace. Others are locked up in prisons and are not even able to see the night sky. (Thanks, Chris, for sharing your heart in this matter.) Many have their bodies wracked with pain because of disease. What about those in Africa and other places who cannot sleep well because they have not had enough to eat? Nighttime is not a good time for those whose bodies and minds cannot rest. They can only lie awake and hope for the coming of light.

Among the sleepless during World War II was a man named Viktor Frankl. A Jew, Frankl was carried away and imprisoned in Auschwitz. As the savagery of the Nazis continued day after day, Frankl watched his body turn into a skeleton. Many around him were killed, and many others just gave up and died. The question of "Why?" was ever-present. Did life still have any meaning? Was there still such a thing as hope for those who were suffering? Frankl later confessed that in the darkness of Auschwitz, he nearly gave up himself.

One particular night, as he stared through the darkness, his vision focused on the barbed wire enclosing his camp, and he wondered why he should go on living. Suicide was such a tempting solution to the pain and emptiness of his life. As his hands clutched the barbed wire, the pain in his soul overflowed, and everything seemed dark and without color. Hopelessness wrapped itself around him like a black blanket. He was at the end of himself, at the end of his strength.

Then, when his tortured mind could stand no more, something caught his eye. Something new was stirring through the darkness. It was the first rays of a new sunrise. In that moment, he said, everything was changed. The rays of that sunrise fought through the darkness of his world, and his despair was dispelled by the light. Hope returned, and he knew somehow that he could withstand the pain and go on a little longer. That sunrise changed his life.

Easter is all about God's power to do for us what that sunrise did for Viktor Frankl. In a world of pain, darkness and sleeplessness when hope falters, the Sonrise reminds us that because of Him everything is changed.

Like the disciples of old who had been fishing fruitlessly in the darkness until they encountered the risen Lord on the beach, the truth of the resurrection enters our world today and turns our empty boats into full ones. The rays of the light of Christ can penetrate the empty darkness and the barbed wire of our existence and restore color to our grayness.

If we truly grasp this, it will make us do wild things, silly things ... things like happily jumping out of a boat and heading across the waves of life toward the shore where Jesus is. On that early morning of Christ's resurrection, Simon Peter knew that from then on nothing would ever be the same. Jesus is alive! And because of Him, so are we.

What are the circumstances of your world? Is your life full of parades, or are you more like Viktor Frankl? My hope is that we turn our eyes beyond the grayness of this world and notice God's light wherever we may find it — in the face of a child or in the words of a friend. May we take time to notice more sunrises and bask in the nightlight of a full moon. May the stars and heavenly bodies remind us of His greatness and glory. And most of all, may the light of the resurrection change everything in our lives, coating us with the knowledge that we are not alone ... that we are loved and valued beyond even the stars and that He conquered death and hell so that we might enjoy eternal victory in Him.

So why are we staying behind in the boat as though He were not raised from the dead? It is time to jump into the cool, fresh waters before us and make for the beach.

After all, Jesus is there, alive and powerful, and He bids us to leave our darkness behind and come have breakfast with Him in the light of a new day.

## 4.5
## Going It Alone

*"... All authority in heaven and on earth has been given to me.*
*Go therefore and make disciples of all nations, baptizing them*
*in the name of the Father and of the Son and of the Holy Spirit,*
*teaching them to observe all that I have commanded you;*
*and lo, I am with you always, to the close of the age."*
– Matthew 28:18–20

How well would you cope if you were all alone for a very long time? Some of us would do better than others. Those among us who are extreme introverts might tend to see time alone as a precious gift. For this group, being alone for short periods would be no hardship at all. Extreme extroverts, on the other hand, would find a long time in solitude akin to torture.

Our personalities and other factors dictate how much time alone we enjoy and how much time we can stand without the company of others. All of us enjoy some time alone. Very few of us, however, would enjoy long periods of being cut off from all others. Some of us would go completely nuts if we were isolated from human contact for very long. Where do you fit in the spectrum?

We once watched a movie based on the life of a boxer called "Hurricane" Carter. Hurricane was a champion boxer until he was accused of murder and imprisoned. At first he had an attitude problem and didn't want to wear a numbered prison uniform like the rest of the prisoners. He flat refused. So he was sent to solitary confinement down in the basement of the prison to "fix" his attitude. He was given 90 days in solitary! Can you imagine being in a dark hole with almost no contact with the outside world for 90 days and nights?

I once had an Uncle "Tootsie" who served time in prison and who was sent to the "hole" (literally a pit down in the ground with an iron grate over it) for a day or two to adjust his attitude. He did all right those couple of days, but I don't think he could have made it 90. Being totally alone would wear most of us down in short order.

Many prisoners of war have spent long stints in solitary confinement. Some, like Sen. John McCain, spent many years without much direct contact with his fellow prisoners, all the while enduring beatings and other terrible hardships. Being kept in isolation is a tactic to break down the person and to make them more willing to trade information for better treatment and more contact with the outside world. Just having others to talk to would certainly help ease some of the pain.

I think about others who have spent long periods alone. Imagine how Charles Lindberg must have felt when he flew his plane over the Atlantic Ocean alone. There was no copilot to take over while he ate, slept or took care of other needs. He was on his own. If he had fallen asleep for long or had engine failure, he would have woken up with the fish of the deep. It was just him and his little airplane all those lonely miles across the Atlantic ... alone.

The Apollo 11 mission went to the moon in July of 1969 with three crewmen aboard: Neil Armstrong, Buzz Aldrin and

105

Michael Collins. Everyone remembers that Armstrong and Aldrin walked on the moon. They were the stars of the show who got most of the glory. In my opinion, though, the role of Michael Collins was the most difficult of all. He stayed behind in the command module *Columbia*, orbiting the moon while Neil and Buzz got to do all the exciting stuff.

Imagine the long hours in space — the Earth on one side and the surface of the moon just below — alone with your thoughts. Even though Collins had some contact with NASA and others via radio, his assignment was a tough one. His solitary vigil must have been very difficult. At least Neil and Buzz had each other in the event that something had gone wrong. Michael had only himself in that module.

When Jesus gave his disciples the commandment that we today call "The Great Commission" in Matthew 28, he instructed us to go, to make disciples, to baptize, to teach and to observe all that He taught. Many of us who call ourselves Christians are trying, in some form or another, to do just that. Some are struggling to do so in very lonely places.

I know how isolated and lonely it can be for pastors serving in the small towns and backwaters of the United States. Church and denominational staff, office workers, people in administration and others can also feel isolated. Some who have almost nothing in common with those they work feel that loneliness. Missionaries who serve in the lonely places of the world without outside help or reinforcements can begin to feel they are attempting an impossible task. (We know something of this feeling after having served in the Amazon Basin, the Outback and the Highlands.) From time to time, many of us may feel we are struggling alone on the dark side of the moon, especially during spiritually dry times. However, our feelings can be wrong.

I have had a growing conviction that many of us are overlooking the best part of the Great Commission. Yes, there is an awful lot of work to be done — much of it in some very lonely places. But we do not have to go it alone.

Jesus said, "... And lo, I am with you always, to the close of the age." I am just foolish enough to believe that He really means every word. If so, can it be that we are never really alone, even when we feel we are? Can it be that in the hardest and most isolated times of our lives and our ministries that He is right there with us, empowering us, sustaining us and enabling us to finish the task?

Could it really be? Yes!

# CHAPTER FIVE

## Discovering Grace

## 5.1
## Missing the Bus
❧

*"See that you do not despise one of these little ones;*
*for I tell you that in heaven their angels always behold*
*the face of my Father who is in heaven. What do you think?*
*If a man has a hundred sheep, and one of them has gone astray,*
*does he not leave the ninety-nine on the mountains and go in search*
*of the one that went astray? And if he finds it, truly, I say to you,*
*he rejoices over it more than over the ninety-nine*
*that never went astray. So it is not the will of my Father*
*who is in heaven that one of these little ones should perish."*
– Matthew 18:10–14

SOMETIMES OUR PLANS WORK like clockwork and things go off without a hitch. Most of the time, however, they don't. It was the poet Robert Burns who said, "The best-laid plans of mice and men are easily laid to waste." Such is the story of a young lady named Meches, who recently came to Xela from Ixchiguan for medical help.

Meches is slightly mentally challenged. Although she has a warm, happy smile, she has had a hard life. As a child she suffered abuse, and her father abandoned her after her mother died. A wonderful lady named Carmen took her in and gave her a place to live and enough food to eat. In exchange, Meches helped cook and clean for the family. It was a good arrangement.

In time, Carmen passed away. Meches had cared for her until the end. Then, some time later, Carmen's husband, Maximo, passed away as well. Again, Meches was there until the bitter end. She may have had limited abilities, but she gave all she had to give, and she gave it willingly. The family of Carmen and Maximo will not easily forget Meches' acts of service.

Therefore, when Meches needed to seek medical help in Xela, her adopted family saw to it that she got the attention she needed. They contacted Lily and asked her to help Meches once she arrived in Xela by taking her to the doctor the next day.

Lily was quite happy to do this and readily agreed. There was just one little problem: Meches couldn't really travel by herself. So a plan was devised whereby Meches would be put on a bus in Ixchiguan, would ride it to San Marcos where she would need to change buses, and then would be met by someone who would ride on with her to Xela. The arrangement sounded simple enough and should have worked. But it didn't.

Meches rode the bus from Ixchiguan to San Marcos without any problems. There people were waiting and watching for her to get off the bus. But for some reason, when Meches arrived in San Marcos, she quickly exited the bus and ducked into a drugstore. Outside, several people looked for her. They called for her in the streets up and down from the terminal. For about three hours, she sat in the store waiting for someone to come inside and find her. All the while, people continued combing the streets looking for her.

Finally, she found our phone number and had the owner of the store talk to Lily. In this way Lily was able to find out exactly where Meches was and relay it to her very frustrated friends. At that point, Carmen and Maximo's son Guayo found his way to Meches and helped her get on the bus to Xela. Guayo asked her why in the world she had darted into a store and hidden there for three hours. But Meches only smiled.

They arrived in Xela with no problems. By that time, however, it had started pouring rain. As they got off the bus at the terminal and prepared to catch another bus, Guayo sternly instructed Meches to stay with him.

"When we get off this bus, we will catch another one that will take us to where we need to go," he explained. "Whatever you do, don't get lost again. Just stay right behind me and do what I do!"

Guayo started to jog through the rain in search for the next bus they needed. There were buses all over the place, and Guayo jogged until he found the right one. He yelled over his shoulder, "This is our bus!"

He boarded and paid the driver for two people. The driver looked at him strangely and asked, "Why do you want to pay for two people since there is only you?"

Guayo jerked around to discover to his horror that Meches was no longer with him! It was almost more than Guayo could take. He jumped off the bus and started calling for Meches and asking if anyone had seen her. Finally one woman pointed to another bus and told him that she had seen the girl who had been with him board another bus. He ran toward the bus just in time to see it pull away … with Meches sitting in a seat by the window. She was still covered in the plastic sheet they had used to try to keep the rain off. Guayo caught a glimpse of her face as the bus pulled away, and she was still smiling.

Guayo ran after the bus screaming for the driver to stop! He didn't. Guayo ran until he could run no more, all the while wondering how Meches would ever find her way back to him.

He was heaving and out of breath and frustrated out of his mind!

It was then that a man drove up and asked Guayo if he needed any help. Quickly Guayo explained the situation, and the two men took off in hot pursuit of the bus. They jigged in and out of traffic in what surely must have looked like a chase scene straight out of the movies. Finally Guayo was able to flag the bus down.

Once the bus was stopped, Guayo rushed aboard and, finding Meches, he chastised her, "Why in the world didn't you stay with me? Why did you go and get on the wrong bus?"

To which Meches replied, "You said that we should get on another bus — so I did!"

"Why didn't you get off once you realized that I did not get on the bus with you?" Guayo asked.

"I just figured that you would catch up later," Meches replied with a smile. "I wasn't worried."

Jesus taught his disciples that the Father is profoundly interested in the little ones. And He is always concerned when one of those little ones goes astray. When one of even the weakest lambs is lost, it is His will that they be found and brought back into the fold. Any action to the contrary would be unacceptable to Him. To not go after them would mean that we are the ones who are "missing the bus!" And that is a very sad thing in the eyes of God!

How does God feel when we don't "pull out all the stops" to help the little ones in need who cross our paths from time to time? There are Mecheses all around us. The problem is that we usually just don't see them. When people are lost — whether they are lost spiritually or just don't know where to turn for help — what does God feel when we don't do everything we can to pursue them? I think that if we really knew the answer to that question, we would run even harder than Guayo to catch up to and bring back those who have gone astray and who are in danger of not being able to find their way home.

The next time you and I see someone who is lost, we ought to do what Jesus wants us to and go running after them. After all, the thought of God's little ones staying lost is just not acceptable!

*Dear Lord, please help us realize how much You care*
*about the "little ones" who are lost, lonely or hurting today.*
*Make us aware of their presence and of their needs*
*in the communities where we live. Give us the courage*
*to go after them. Though it requires much from us,*
*please give us the strength to persevere until we see*
*these little ones safely enter into the folds of God.*
*For this is Your will through Jesus Christ our Lord*
*in whose name we pray.*
*Amen.*

## 5.2
## Dropping the Lowest Grade

*The scribes and the Pharisees brought a woman*
*who had been caught in adultery, and placing her in the midst*
*they said to him, "Teacher, this woman has been caught*
*in the act of adultery. Now in the law Moses commanded us*
*to stone such. What do you say about her?"*
*… And as they continued to ask him, he stood up and said to them,*
*"Let him who is without sin among you be the first to throw a stone*
*at her." … But when they heard it, they went away, one by one,*
*beginning with the eldest, and Jesus was left alone with the woman*
*standing before him …. Jesus looked up and said to her,*
*"Woman, where are they? Has no one condemned you?"*
*She said, "No one, Lord." And Jesus said,*
*"Neither do I condemn you; go, and do not sin again."*
*– John 8:3–5, 7, 9–11*

SOME TIME AGO while we were on stateside assignment, we had
to make a trip back to Guatemala during November and
December in order to survey the disaster in our area caused by
Hurricane Stan. When we returned to South Carolina, our son,
Will, had to do quite a bit of catching up on his schoolwork. One
of his assignments was to download an article on something in
the news that related to his biology class. As he was preparing
to turn it in, however, he ran into another classmate who had
already failed to turn in one current event article and who was

frantic because he had forgotten about the second one as well. Will, having the tender heart that he does, decided that his friend needed the article worse than he did, and so he took off his cover page and handed the article over to his friend. Because of the nature of the assignment, Will was in no way cheating, and we were pleased with his giving spirit, but we were concerned about what would happen if he didn't have enough time to do another one.

"Son," we told him, "you have to do another one right away and turn it in tomorrow so you won't have a zero on your record."

"It's okay," he informed us. "I talked to my teacher today, and he told me that he had already planned to drop the lowest current events grade anyway."

As I thought about Will being able to drop his lowest grade, several memories flooded through my head of times when I had really blown it and someone chose to forgive me and allowed me to, in effect, drop the lowest grades of my life.

I could easily tell you of many other instances in my life (I shudder to even think about them!) when others have forgiven me and wiped the slate clean even though I was as guilty as I could be. Grace has always been an amazing thing to me! What a remarkable thing it is to be forgiven and have your lowest grade dropped — even when you know you don't deserve it.

When Jesus came face to face with the obvious sin of a woman caught in the very act of adultery, the crowd of teachers and Pharisees around Him wanted to stone the woman on the spot! After all, she was obviously guilty, and they would probably get some kind of perverse thrill out of condemning her. Isn't it interesting how good human beings can be at passing judgment?

A few years ago I had been talking with an American Catholic priest in our area of Guatemala. The man had developed a theory that every sickness of man is somehow related to the blood. He tied it theologically to the shedding of Christ's blood for us because he believed illnesses were due to tainted blood. You would not be surprised to learn that he advocated blood transfusions for almost any illness.

I thought the guy was a little strange, and I certainly disagreed with him theologically on many levels. This same priest, though, in spite of his weird ideas, was involved in reaching out to the poor and helping the sick and the homeless, and he got involved in every way he could to improve the life of his parishioners. I will never forget the discussion I had with a gas station attendant who knew the priest fairly well. I commented that although the priest obviously did a lot of good, he was very far out there in his blood theories. As I pointed out this one striking fault, the gas station attendant looked over at my shirt, picked a little piece of lint off, and looked at me with a glint in his eye. Then he picked another off. I quickly understood what he was saying to me. Who was I to nitpick this well-intentioned priest? Other theological differences aside, why couldn't I just overlook this "lowest grade" in his personality? Why did I have to run him down to the gas station attendant rather than focus on some of the other good and wonderful things he was doing?

It is so much easier to identify the worst qualities of everyone else, even when they have many good ones. It's somehow our nature to be judgmental, critical, and ready to accuse others for their faults. What would the world be like, though, if we could be learn to do as Jesus did and pardon people's mistakes, offering them a new chance to get it right? What if we, like Will's biology teacher, could learn to daily "drop the lowest grade" of those around us? How would others respond to us and to the gospel if we became forgiving people? What if we were loving and so thankful for the forgiveness we ourselves have received that we were ready to liberally pass it out to others in order to encourage them to go and sin no more?

I have made it one of my goals to try to be a little less judgmental and nitpicking. I want to try to be more like Jesus and to forgive the obvious faults of others — in the hope that they will do the same for me. I want to be a carrier of grace and not so much a deliverer of judgment and condemnation. I want to drop the lowest grade of those around me and focus less on what they're doing wrong and more on what they're trying to do right. God will judge all of us; He doesn't need me for this particular job! Instead, He simply asks me to point others to the source of all forgiveness: the Lord Jesus Christ. I would like to do a better job of that.

So, are there any others out there who would be interested in joining me in laying down the rocks we have stockpiled to stone one another with? We actually have the chance to make the world a little better by living out grace and forgiveness, which is so different from trying to be the judge, jury and executioner for all the sinners in the world who are in fact a whole lot like us!

Think about it!

## 5.3
## A New Name

*...[Y]ou shall be called by a new name*
*which the mouth of the Lord will give.*
– Isaiah 62:2b

*"...I will give him a white stone, with a new name written*
*on the stone which no one knows except him who receives it."*
– Revelation 2:17b

OVER THE YEARS, we have known some people with some interesting names. My hometown of Williamston, South Carolina, had some doozies: Tootsie, Wootsie, Tiny, Doc, Datche, Big Hap, Little Hap, Nub, J.E., Bonehead, Spook, Sunset, Banana Eater, Milledge, Tersh and Bobo. Yes, Williamston is a colorful little town!

In college we had a female friend called Boo. Her husband was named Macon, and sometimes we inadvertently juxtaposed their initial letters, calling them "Moo and Bacon." Another friend had the real name of Kansas City — that's the way it read on his birth certificate! (He asked us all to please just call him K.C.) In Australia we knew an aboriginal man named Electric Motor. That even beat the name of the chief of the Katherine Walpiri tribe. It was Lewis Lewis (not to be shortened to Louie Louie!). In Guatemala we work with a man named Dolores,

119

which means "pains." He has a brother named Fecundo, which means "fertile." We are too frightened to ask their sister's name!

I myself am the proud owner of "Trenton" as my middle name. (Yep, as in Trenton, New Jersey.) My brother, Steve, as a 4-year-old, heard the name during a radio news show and asked if I could be named that. (Thanks a lot, Steve! Why my parents listened to you, we will never know!) I like my first name much better, and I have my mother to thank for it. "Gary" is supposed to mean something like "faithful warrior." I would like to think that I am a faithful warrior of the Lord. At least it is something to try to live up to … and it sure beats Electric Motor!

Our name can be either a blessing or a curse. While some people go through life disliking their name, others are proud of theirs and see a family heritage or a family hope built in their name. I was almost named David. That was my father's choice, but my mother's won out. David, as we all know, was the name of Israel's great king who was a "man after God's own heart." That's not bad, either! It's certainly a good example of a name that can take a lifetime to grow into.

The Bible speaks of God giving us new names. I like that, don't you? Just as Jesus told Nicodemus that we all must be born again, God changes our identities. In Him we truly are new creatures with new personalities and even new names. In Him we are capable of making an impact on our world that would have been impossible before we met Him. Our whole outlook is changed, and we begin to see ourselves as an instrument in His service rather than merely an isolated person born on the planet.

I really like the words to a song used by Centrifuge and written by a man named D.J. Butler (whose parents also must have had a sense of humor) called "I Will Change Your Name."

*I will change your name.*
*You shall no longer be called*
*Wounded, Outcast, Lonely or Afraid.*
*I will change your name.*
*Your new name shall be*
*Confidence, Joyfulness, Overcoming One*
*Faithfulness, Friend of God,*
*One Who Seeks My Face.*

Whatever your birth certificate may say about your name, your real name in Him is something better. By His transforming grace, each of us has been given a new identity — one that we will take a lifetime to grow into. So hold your head up (even if you were named "Bonehead" by your strange, original parents). Your real Father has given you a new name, a beautiful name ... for we are now the sons and daughters of God.

Let us live our lives growing up as Confidence, Joyfulness, Overcoming One, Faithfulness, Friend of God, and One Who Seeks His Face.

## 5.4
## A Tale of Spit and Dirt
❦

*And Elisha sent a messenger to him [Naaman], saying,*
*"Go and wash in the Jordan seven times, and your flesh*
*shall be restored, and you shall be clean."*
*But Naaman was angry, and went away, saying,*
*"I thought that he would surely come out to me, and stand,*
*and call on the name of the Lord his God, and wave his hand over*
*the place, and cure the leper. Are not Abana and Pharpar, the rivers*
*of Damascus, better than all the waters of Israel?"*
– 2 Kings 5:10–12a

---

*As [Jesus] passed by, he saw a man blind from his birth.*
...
*... [H]e spat on the ground and made clay of the spittle*
*and anointed the man's eyes with the clay, saying to him,*
*"Go, wash in the pool of Siloam" (which means Sent).*
*So he went and washed and came back seeing.*
...
*"[O]ne thing I know, that though I was blind, now I see."*
– John 9:1, 6b–7, 25b

AT TIMES OUR HAPPINESS DEPENDS not upon the circumstances
we have been handed but rather upon what we make of them. It
is an irony of life that many people who have the most in terms
of what this world values are the most unhappy, while others
who have the least are truly happy.

Have you ever thought about this? Why is that many people who have so much to celebrate are miserable? And why are there some who have almost nothing to celebrate (that we can see) are happy, content and thankful for their many blessings? In short, it is all about our attitude and our willingness to use wisely what we have instead of wasting our days complaining and wishing for what we don't have. It reflects on our faith in God and our trust in Him as we face both the abundance and the abasement that come with living.

In the passages on the previous page, we have an interesting contrast between men with two very different attitudes and perspectives. In the first passage, we see Naaman, commander of the army of the king of Syria, with all of his pride and self-importance, getting angry at the instructions of the prophet Elisha. Naaman had but one problem. He had leprosy. Other than that, his life was going great.

When he sought help for this one area of need, he found himself being instructed to wash himself seven times in the Jordan River (which to him was a foreign, dirty river not nearly as nice as those he was accustomed to in Syria). He was incensed. He expected more pizzazz … more hocus-pocus. Instead what he got was a common prescription that he considered beneath him. Had it not been for his servant, who talked him into doing what the prophet said, he would have remained a leper all his days.

In the second passage from the book of John, we find a man who also had a problem. But his problem was one of many. He had been blind since birth. Unlike Naaman, he had no issue of pride to deal with. He was blind and never expected to regain his sight. When Jesus came into his experience, he did not become resentful. He did not take offense ... even when the Lord spat in the dirt, made a mud pie, and then rubbed it in his eyes. (How many of us would accept someone rubbing their spit and dirt into our eyes? *Just a minute there, Lord! You want to do what? You want to spit in the dirt AND THEN RUB IT IN MY EYES?*)

The blind man could have gotten offended and reprimanded the Lord for treating him in such a base way. He didn't, though. Just the opposite. He gladly did what the Lord instructed and was grateful that God had worked in his life. "One thing I know," he said, "that though I was blind, now I see." He had no trouble accepting that God's plan was infinitely better than anything else he had going on in his life. His attitude was one of gratitude.

And so it goes. Some people who have every reason to be grateful become bitter and resentful and wish to say "no" to God's plan in their lives. Their circumstances are not what they asked for, and they cannot understand why they are not given something better — much better! While this lot is complaining, there are others who can see God working even in the "spit and dirt" of life. And more than that, they are even grateful for the grace that they have been given. And that is a rare gift indeed.

Once upon a time, I had the privilege of working with two men. One had a business making lots of money. He lived in an expensive house and had a beautiful wife and healthy children. In terms of material blessings, he was way ahead of most people. However, he was miserable and always wanted more. His pride was easily offended, and he always looked around to see others getting what he felt he was entitled to. I once heard him pray, "Lord, please bless us according to our merits." (God forbid!)

124

The other man made a lot less money. His house was not as big or as expensive as the first man's, but it was nice enough and always felt like home. He too was blessed with a wonderful family, but his wife suffered from an illness that kept her in constant pain. In spite of that, however, she was always concerned for others and considered their troubles worse than her own. She spent her time praying for them and, when she could, cooked dishes for others when they were sick. Her husband suffered a stroke during this time. He had so many things he could have complained about. However, I will never forget a prayer meeting in the church when we had a "choose your favorite hymn" night. In the midst of all his trouble, would you like to guess which hymn he wanted to sing?

> *Count your blessings,*
> *Name them one by one,*
> *Count your many blessings,*
> *See what God has done!*

Gratitude, not bitterness, filled his heart and kept his eyes focused on the love of God that was revealed in his life.

It comes back to attitude, and attitude is a matter of choice. No circumstance can make us happy, and no circumstance can make us bitter … unless we allow it. The choice is ours and ours alone. Whom do we choose to be like: Naaman the prideful leper, or the humble blind man who gratefully received his sight from the Lord? (Can we really get to the point where we will be grateful for even spit and dirt? I sure hope so … .)

> *Lord, today do You want to moisten a little dirt*
> *with Your spit and then rub it into our eyes that we*

*might see? If that is what You want to do, then bring it on!*
*We have no better plan. Spit and dirt are fine with us,*
*if it comes from You. Feel free to do with us*
*whatever seems good to You.*
*While You're at it, Lord, please help us change our attitude*
*to one of gratitude and teach us to count our many blessings*
*that we might truly see what You are about in our lives.*
*For to see and to understand Your will ... that is where*
*our true contentment lies — regardless of the circumstances*
*that may come our way.*
*Amen.*

## 5.5
## The Faces of Grace

*But by the grace of God I am what I am,*
*and his grace toward me was not in vain.*
– 1 Corinthians 15:10a

*Law came in, to increase the trespass;*
*but where sin increased, grace abounded all the more ... .*
– Romans 5:20

IT HAPPENED ABOUT 5:30 one morning in the darkness, framed by the quiet street that runs like a stream in front of our house. I worked quickly to accomplish what had to be done.

Black bags in hand, I bundled up each item that I had carried to our front gate. There were broken things, forgotten things and unwanted things in my stash. There were things that had been kept for far too long in the storage building in our backyard, such as a broken chair, old paint cans, rat-chewed cardboard, and old parts for cars that we no longer even owned. Cracked wooden pieces, rusty metal parts and broken plastic items populated the pile. All in all, what came out of our shed was, at its best, only filthy trash.

But then a wonderful thing took place! A truck came by, and three men got out and loaded up all our garbage and hauled it away. When I took another look at about 7 a.m., I could see only green grass where my garbage had been. What a marvelous thing it was to receive such a gift!

A few years ago a thief was caught in Ixchiguan. Stealing was common where we lived, and I, along with others in our community, rejoiced to see somebody actually get caught! The person caught had been hauling away firewood and crops belonging to a neighbor. Several of us shook our heads and marveled at the audacity of a young boy who would be so bold as to steal things in broad daylight!

His name was Chebo, and this was not the first time he had been caught stealing, we found out. He had started young. His mother had died, and his father despised him. Not a very good start in life.

Chebo was caught red-handed by a neighbor, who promptly hauled him into town and formally charged him before the town police. The police were happy to have this thief apprehended as well. But as they started hearing the whole story, they were not as happy as they thought they would be. Chebo did steal from his neighbor, but he stole raw potatoes out of the ground because he was hungry! Without a mother or a father to look after him, he had to scrounge for food as best he could. He was caught eating the only thing he could find, and for that he was hauled to justice.

As Chebo was being charged, a little boy listened in to his story and felt sorry for him. This little boy went back home and talked his father, who was not usually the compassionate sort, into rescuing little Chebo. For a little while, Chebo was allowed to live with the family who had rescued him, and for a while Chebo had enough food to eat so that he did not have to dig potatoes out of the ground and eat them raw. For a little while,

Chebo found grace — not from me (not at first, anyway) and not from most of the people in our community — but from a little boy and a heathen father who chose to show grace to a needy boy who wasn't even his.

I remember once as a young boy stealing a pair of scissors (go figure) from a store. No one dragged me before the police. My mother took me back to the store and had me return them with an apology, but that was the end of it. No lockup, no police cell awaiting me ... just the quiet correction of a loving mother intent only on teaching me right from wrong. Unlike Chebo's experience, I had a family who loved me. My mother's face was, for me, the face of grace and of forgiveness.

I think back to another time and another place. I was in grammar school, and for some unknown reason it occurred to me to write a letter filled with the dirtiest words I knew and pass it to a friend of mine. On the way to my friend, however, it was intercepted by my teacher. I knew that I was fried! She opened up my letter, read it, and then folded it back and just looked at me. I hung my head in shame, realizing I could not even begin to marshal a defense for such a stupid act. I was guilty, plain and simple!

As I awaited sentencing, my teacher asked what I thought she should do about the letter.

"Should we show this to your Mom and Dad?" she asked.

"No ma'am," I replied softly with fear rising up in my throat.

After a moment of silence, she told me that she had made her decision. "I'll tell you what I am going to do," she said. "I am going to tear this note up — this time. But I expect to never see another note like this from you ever again! Is that understood?"

"Yes, ma'am," I quickly replied, hardly daring to believe my good fortune. As I looked at the face of my teacher, I saw once again "the face of grace."

As we come to terms with the reality of our existence and with all the terrible things that we have done in our lives, some of us realize that we probably should have run out of second chances long ago. We have been given much more grace and forgiveness than we deserve, and yet we have given much less grace and forgiveness than others have deserved from us.

From time to time we are reminded that God has been merciful to us. Instead of judging or dealing as harshly with us as we deserve, He reveals the sweetest face of grace ever imagined. When we were undeserving, He gave us His only begotten Son to look upon so that we might know what grace is all about. Just imagine. The God of the entire universe, with all His power and with all His glory, chose to reveal His great mercy to us through a tiny little baby named Jesus! And it was through this baby, who grew up to be our Savior and who would die in our place on a tree, that we really get a glimpse of the love of God.

It was Jesus, after all, who would act to take all our garbage away in the night, was it not? It was Jesus who would feel compassion for the poor and the needy and actually do something to help them instead of condemning them! And it was Jesus who would tear up the papers with all our vile sins written upon them and whisper softly to us, "Go and sin no more." Jesus is God's face of grace that assures us of God's great love for us and of His forgiveness of all our sins.

Since God has done so much for us, shouldn't we be the face of grace for someone else? Shouldn't we mirror God's love so that someone else might see Him and His grace?

Think about it. Better yet, just go out and do it! Both you and the world will be glad you did.

# CHAPTER SIX

## Finding Forgiveness

## 6.1
## Of Mud and Briars

*Again Jesus spoke to them, saying, "I am the light of the world;*
*he who follows me will not walk in darkness,*
*but will have the light of life."*
– John 8:12

*... [T]he sheep hear his voice, and he calls his own sheep*
*by name and leads them out. When he has brought out all his own,*
*he goes before them, and the sheep follow him,*
*for they know his voice.*
– John 10:3–4

A FEW YEARS AGO, we had the opportunity to take a few days
away from our normal routines and spend some time on a
father-son retreat up in the northern part of Guatemala. There
were 15 of us in all, and we headed for a camp on a remote farm
called Chi Melb in Alta Vera-Paz. I had been there once several
years before and fondly remembered the place. We all planned
to camp in a shelter built on the top of a hill that overlooks a
beautiful horseshoe-shaped lake. The lake wraps around the hill,
making it a short trip from the shelter to the water. With great
fishing opportunities, the place was, in my mind, a paradise.

But things change. When we arrived, the whole place was
overgrown with weeds, bushes and briars. The owners had let
the place go, and it was overrun with undergrowth. Recent rains

had turned everything into soupy mud. Worst of all, the dam controlling the exit of the water from the lake had been opened up, shrinking the lake to a fraction of its former size. Access to the waterfront was now covered in mud and briars, making it almost inaccessible, and the shelter overlooking it all was now a long hike from the water.

Nevertheless, we set about cleaning out the shelter in preparation for pitching our tents under its metal roof. Then we headed down the hill with our rods-and-reels and one cane pole (mine) in hand. As we made our way toward the lake, the rains started again. Soon our shoes were mired in mud while briars tore at our clothes and skin. When we finally reached our fishing spot among the rocks, Will's reel wouldn't work, and someone (yours truly) knocked over our tackle box, spilling all our hooks, weights and lures. Needless to say, we didn't catch any fish that night. We finally gave up and made our way back up the hill just before dark.

Another group of us had gone down the other side of the hill to fish. As darkness fell, most of them had also made their way back to our shelter, but two boys, Andrew and Cam, had chosen to stay out a little later.

We all got cleaned up as best we could and prepared to have supper (in lieu of the fish fry we had planned). As we got things ready, we noticed that Andrew and Cam were still not back. Their fathers called out in the darkness for them to come up the hill and eat. No response. After several yells, we heard their voices on the opposite end of the farm. Hoping to avoid the mud and the briars on the way back up, they had tried another trail. In the darkness, they didn't realize it didn't lead them home. They were lost far from our shelter.

We called out to them to look for our flashlights and lanterns on the hill and encouraged them to keep focused on our light and to listen to their father's voice. They had to backtrack down to the lake again and make their way back through the mud and the briars in order to get back home. Finally they made it and were safe once again.

I couldn't help but think of the parallels in our walk with Christ. How many times have we chosen to stay behind in the darkness and then lost the trail back home, wandering in the mud and briars of sin? How many times have we taken another trail, hoping that it would lead us to where we wanted, only to find that we must go back, through the mud and briars, and take the true path? We call this repentance. Like Andrew and Cam, we too have been rescued many times, but only because we refocused on the light of Christ and strained hard to hear our Father's voice leading us to the right path. We've all been there and done that, haven't we?

The Bible teaches us that God's sheep will hear and recognize His voice and that He will lead us. There is no doubt about that. The only question is whether or not we will follow Him closely.

Whether on a daily basis deciding how best to be faithful in the things that we do, or on a much larger scale of our life's work and the really big decisions of our lives, we can get sidetracked at times and begin to wander. But we must remember that our Father keeps His eye on us even when we take our eyes off Him. He calls to us lovingly, and He shines His light through Jesus so that we can see the trails that He wants us to walk — the trails that will lead us back to His shelter and back into His service.

Are we where we need to be today, doing what God has called us to? Or are we sidetracked in the mud and the briars of life trying to follow our own way? Regardless, if we stop and listen very carefully, we will hear our Father's voice. If we look in His direction, He will give us the light we need through Christ to get on and to stay on the right trail.

Tired of getting torn up fighting briars and mud? Let's get on the right trail and head toward home.

Our Father already has supper ready.

## 6.2
## Bridges to a Better Understanding of Forgiveness
🍂

*Surely he has borne our griefs and carried our sorrows;*
*yet we esteemed him stricken, smitten by God, and afflicted.*
*But he was wounded for our transgressions,*
*he was bruised for our iniquities;*
*upon him was the chastisement that made us whole,*
*and with his stripes we are healed.*
– Isaiah 53:4–5

So MANY PEOPLE HEAR the gospel but just don't get it. They hear about God's love for them, about the consequences of their sins, and about God's plan to redeem them through Jesus. Sadly, it seems to make no sense to them. Coming from broken lives with negative role models and negative experiences, they don't seem to be able to comprehend what it all means. Their eyes are blinded and their ears are deaf. That is ... until God builds a bridge for them to be able to grasp the meaning of the death and resurrection of His Son. And that is always an amazing event!

What "bridges" has God built in your life in order for you to be able to understand the gospel? Some of you will find it hard to think of any "bridges" right away. But if you will continue to think about it, I am sure you will remember events that helped you or even made it possible for you to understand enough to believe.

Of course, one of the reasons that we have a hard time identifying those bridges is that they seemed to be such ordinary, everyday events. Only in looking back are we able to see them for what they truly were: God's bridges that made it possible for us to understand we could put our faith and trust in Him!

The story that I am going to share with you is terrible, and I am ashamed of it now — but I wasn't when it happened. In looking back, I am positive that it was a bridge sent from God so that I, an angry, scarred, confused little boy, would later comprehend what Jesus did for me on the cross. It was through some strange experiences that God allowed my warped mind to begin to understand what forgiveness is really all about.

I grew up in a dysfunctional family. Alcoholism, uncontrolled anger and immature thinking caused much of my family at large to be severely emotionally and spiritually handicapped. I grew up in this environment on a little mill hill in South Carolina. The church was non-existent to our pagan family. We just didn't get it — perhaps could not get it — and the church apparently did not know how to relate to us, either. I had many issues with anger and blame for all the wrongs in my life. Somehow my brother Steve became the focus of this anger. He was an easy mark; he loved me, and I trusted him enough to dump all my feelings on him, knowing that no matter what I did, he would still love me. (I wish with all my soul that everyone had a "Brother Steve!")

One day my anger was at a boiling point, and I screamed at Steve, telling him that he always "picked on me" and that he never treated me right! He and I both knew that this was a lie, but it was a convenient lie. Steve was about 16, and I was about 12. I went on and on, telling him how unfair and unjust his treatment of me was. (Perhaps this was a condensation of all my anger at the world at large or even at God, conveniently rolled up into one attack against my brother.)

Steve listened to all my complaints about him and saw my fury grow and grow. Then he asked me, "Do you really believe what you are saying — that I have treated you wrong your whole life?"

"Yes I do!" I screamed at him.

He just stared at me, knowing that I had gone completely over the edge. "If you really believe what you are saying — that I have never treated you right — then I'll tell you what I'm going to do," he said. "I am going to stand here before you and make it right by letting you hit me three times — anywhere on my body that you want — and I swear that I won't do anything back to you after you have hit me."

"You swear?" I asked with uncertainty.

"I swear!" he said again.

Steve took my first punch. I think I hit him in the stomach. It hurt him, but he could take it. After a moment, he shook it off and said, "Okay, punch number two … ."

This time I hit him in the face as hard as I could. It must have hurt badly, but he stood it and got control of himself again.

"Number three … ."

This time I put everything I had into my punch. I hit him on the jaw so furiously that I knocked him to the ground.

Suddenly my rage ended, replaced by blind fear as I realized what I had just done. I knew that he had every right to get up off that ground and kill me!

Steve got up, looked at me, and walked away. With my fist hurting quite a bit, I simply stood still and tried to process what

140

had just happened. My only brother, whom I knew to be innocent, had been falsely accused by me, and he had responded by letting me take my three best punches on his body. Then as he got up off the ground, he forgave me, (Indeed, I believe that he had already forgiven me before he hit the ground.) and left me, taking away my rage and proclaiming me guiltless. I could not believe it. I just could not believe it!

I did not know it that day, but God, through my brother, had provided a bridge to my understanding of Jesus. While I could not possibly process all that had just happened, I was able to understand even then that my innocent brother had taken all that I could dish out and had fallen to the ground because of me and that he had risen from the ground already having forgiven me! It was an example of love beyond my comprehension! It was an example that would later provide a bridge to my understanding what Christianity was all about.

It would be several more months before I would hear the gospel for the first real time and before I would commit my life to the Lord.

It was even later when I more fully came to grips with the result of my sinfulness that put three nails into Jesus' body and that knocked Him to the ground with the heaviness of bearing my guilt and shame. Even today, I grapple with understanding Jesus' bearing our sins and not holding us accountable for them anymore … for loving us and preparing a place for us in heaven so that we might be with Him for all eternity! For us — even after what we did to Him! It will take me all eternity to even begin to contemplate all that means. But for now, I can at least begin to understand it … because of the bridge that God provided for me through my brother.

I would wish that God would provide for you a Brother Steve, so that you might know more intimately what Jesus has done for you. I also wish with all my heart that both you and I might be used of God to be "brother Steve bridges" for someone else — so that they might also come to understand in a hands-on way what Jesus has done for them!

Selah (let it be so), Lord! Selah!

## 6.3
## Climbing the Next Step

*So speak and so act as those who are to be judged under the law
of liberty. For judgment is without mercy to one who has shown
no mercy; yet mercy triumphs over judgment.*
– James 2:12–13

I REMEMBER AS A LITTLE BOY playing a game that we called
"Going Up to Heaven." It was played on a set of stairs where
there were usually six or eight steps, with one person sitting on
an upper step and all the other children seated on lower ones.
The person above would usually put both hands behind his back
and hide a rock in one of them. Then both hands would be
presented to one person at a time. If that person correctly chose
the hand with the rock in it, he or she would move up one step.
If he chose incorrectly, he would have to retreat a step. The
person directing the game would try to get everyone to goof up
and keep them on the lower steps because it was fun to be the
leader and stay on the top step as long as possible.

Sometime ago I had a very different experience. I was in a
little mall in Xela, and I couldn't help but notice an older
indigenous woman who stood staring up at the new escalator
that had been built in order to make it easier to get to the second
floor of the mall. The escalator moved continually, and the lady

was frightened and unsure as to exactly how to go up the thing, and yet she clearly wanted to. Without thinking much about it, I volunteered to help. I explained very simply how to step on and then demonstrated by doing so first. I offered my hand to steady her as she placed her foot on the first step. She took my hand and held on as though I were the only thing between her and death itself.

She giggled almost hysterically as we rode to the top floor. At the top she leapt off and thanked me profusely. I was glad to have helped and felt confident that the next time she wanted to, she would be able to take the escalator by herself (probably still giggling wildly, though).

These different experiences got me to thinking: (1) Why do we as Christians take more delight in sitting on the top steps watching and criticizing those who are not as high up as we think we are, and (2) why aren't we doing more to take people's hands to help them up the next step in front of them?

The difference in these two approaches is extreme!

There is also another factor. We often try to exhort people to move straight up to where we are without remembering how many little steps we ourselves had to travel to get to where we now are. Is it really practical that we should tell someone that God expects them to live on the top steps when they are still trying to figure out how, for instance, to stop drinking or how to read their Bibles?

Several simple lessons stand out in my mind:

1. It seems so clear that we need to spend a whole lot more time being practical in helping folks move up one step at a time to a better place in their lives instead of staying on our top steps exhorting them to hurry up and get up there.

2. We can help others so much more by taking the time to hold their hands and teach them how to begin upward motion in their lives. They don't need to be so concerned yet about how to get to the top step (which may have cost us many years of prayer, discipleship, and experience in Christian service, as well as high school, college, seminary training and much more). What they most need is someone who can take their hand and help them first face, and then climb, that one step in front of them. After that, they can concentrate on the next step, and then the next, and the next ... .

People feel our criticisms — the way we look down upon them, and our higher-up-than-thou attitudes — and they resent them. But few will complain if we get down where they are, take their hand in ours, and walk with them up the next step. And then, one day when they are ready, we can help them take the next.

This is the kind of help that makes the world stand up and take notice. It is the kind of gospel that people will recognize as helpful and that they will appreciate as much as the little lady who learned to negotiate an escalator one day. Not all steps may lead to that kind of steep growth, but each step up is one step more in following God's plan for their lives.

Anyone interested in "Going Up to Heaven"? Jesus is offering His hand of salvation. Why, then, should we not offer our hands to lift up others to the next step in front of them? After all, that is exactly what countless followers of Christ have done over the years to help us to get where we are! Or have we forgotten that little fact already?

So go on. Take that hand and help someone who doesn't know what to do next discover the joy of climbing up and overcoming the step that has been holding them back for so long!

Now that's growth!

## 6.4
## What Do We Want Him To Do for Us?

*And Jesus stopped, and commanded him*
*to be brought to him; and when he came near, he asked him,*
*"What do you want me to do for you?"*
*He said, "Lord, let me receive my sight." And Jesus said*
*to him, "Receive your sight; your faith has made you well."*
– Luke 18:40–42

THIS PASSAGE HAS ALWAYS PUZZLED me. I've read it so many times, and I have also watched this scene in the "Jesus Film" umpteen dozens of times.

This poor blind man is waiting along the road when Jesus and his disciples pass by. He asks those around him what all the commotion is about, and someone tells him that Jesus of Nazareth is passing. He has heard that name before. He knows that this is the young man whom everyone is talking about: teacher, healer, miracle worker. This teacher might be the very thing he has been hoping for. So he begins to cry out, begging the Son of David to have mercy on him.

Those around him become annoyed with his pleas and tell him to shut up! He yells all the more, getting even more desperate. When he finally gets Jesus' attention, the Son of God looks into his face and asks him a simple question: "What do you want Me to do for you?"

So many times I have wondered why in the world Jesus asked him that. Duh! The guy is blind as a bat! His need is so obvious! What blind man does not want his sight back? Why would Jesus even need to ask? Yet that is precisely what Jesus wants to know: "What do you want Me to do for you?"

Several years ago, we worked with a team from Spartanburg, South Carolina, doing medical clinics. During that week, we also had a request to go into another village called Tuiquinamble, about 15 minutes away. One particular family was begging for help, and when they heard that we had two doctors on the team, they pleaded for someone to bring the doctors to attend them.

When we got to the house, we found two situations. The father introduced us to his son, who was lying in bed aching all over and could not get up or do anything for himself. Then he introduced us to his daughter, who lay blind upon her hard bed in a hut next door. They had tried witch doctors and medicines of many kinds to help the two, to no avail. Now they were asking the Lord, through us, for help. Fortunately, the doctors were able to diagnose the son and get him the medicine that he needed to battle rheumatoid arthritis. We prayed for spiritual and physical help for him. We prayed also for the blind daughter and gave her vitamins to make her stronger.

Within a few days, the son was out of bed and feeling like a new man. The vitamins helped the daughter, and she too was feeling much better (even though her blindness remained). The father was so grateful that he promised to follow Christ and wanted to be part of starting a Christian church in his village.

After several weeks the children were both still doing much better. However, the father reconsidered his offer to accept

Christ as his Savior. He decided that he really did not want to follow Christ. Things seemed fine just the way they were. *Just fix our bodies and leave our souls alone! Patch us up and we'll be fine … .*

At last I think I am getting a clearer understanding of Jesus' question to the blind man: "What do you want Me to do for you?" Is He not saying, "What do you want to be like when we finish here?" Jesus offered physical healing to many people. He could easily take care of blindness, paralysis, and so many other maladies that trouble people. But He offered more — so, so much more than just physical help!

We have always wanted help, but we are so blind that what we ask for is usually only the physical. We ask God to help us with our health, money, physical protection, solutions to our outward problems, and so on. We may give token pleas for "a closer walk with Jesus," but the bulk of our asking usually focuses on physical, verifiable, "fix it" or "fix me" kinds of help.

What would our lives be like if we hungered for spiritual help more than we desired physical help? What if our pleas were for complete wholeness, so much so that we would be transformed into the image of Christ?

Imagine if we prayed, *Lord, I am so broken inside. Please humble me and remake me totally so that I have more compassion for others.* Or how about, *Lord, today let me be like Jesus, a man of sorrows and acquainted with grief so that I might be an instrument of Your grace to others.* What would life be like if we focused on our spiritual blindness so much that we forgot to mention our physical requests until the end of our prayers?

Perhaps Jesus is still looking into our faces as He asks us the same question that He asked the blind man so long ago: "What do you want Me to do for you?"

It is still a haunting question.

# 6.5
## Receiving the Cross

*For the word of the cross is folly to those who are perishing,*
*but to us who are being saved it is the power of God.*
– 1 Corinthians 1:18

*But we impart a secret and hidden wisdom of God,*
*which God decreed before the ages for our glorification.*
*None of the rulers of this age understood this;*
*for if they had, they would not have crucified the Lord of glory.*
– 1 Corinthians 2:7–8

THE CROSS IS FUNDAMENTAL to the understanding of the Christian faith. If you don't understand the cross, you don't understand Christianity. To distort or do away with the significance of the death of Christ on Calvary's cross is to lose the essence of our salvation.

Yet it is precisely at the point of the cross that so many stumble. While some deny their sinfulness and their need to be forgiven, thus making the death of Christ unnecessary, others deny that Jesus really died on the cross. The doctrine of the cross, for so many in our world, is just downright hard to accept. The significance of the cross is truly a "secret and hidden wisdom of God" to those who have not yet believed.

It is interesting that the symbol of the cross has been used by other cultures for thousands of years. I remember walking

151

around in southern England many years ago and seeing the Druid crosses in ancient fields. The crosses had been put there long before Jesus ever came to this planet to be born. Other cultures have used it as well.

Jesus didn't hold the copyright on the cross. The devil had already used it down through the ages as a symbol of torture and death. Jesus requisitioned and adopted the cross and gave it God's salvific meaning. No one else could have used something so awful and turned it into something so beautiful: a sign of our complete forgiveness and salvation! As the saying goes, "often imitated but never duplicated." Still, so many in our world don't understand that.

We once had the opportunity to listen to stories from one of our sisters in a new work area in Mam country. She shared with us that she had recently been invited to attend an initiation ritual for spiritists (*espiritistas*), Mayan priests (*chimanes*) and witch doctors (*brujos*) — all distinct categories, mind you. She hesitated to go but decided in the end that she was confident enough in her own salvation and relationship with the Lord that watching the rituals could not hurt her but might help her to understand what we're up against. So she went. Later she described how she had made her way with a large group of people down to the river on the given day. There on the riverbank those awaiting passage to becoming full-fledged Mayan priests were exhorted to do two things: to receive the cross and to be baptized.

Isn't it fascinating that they were exhorted to "receive the cross"? Please understand that this had absolutely nothing to do with Christianity. They were not being asked to receive Jesus into their hearts — far from it. They were being asked to receive

152

the commission of becoming mediators between the spirit world and those who would pay them to perform sacrifices of candles, incense, alcohol, corn, turkey eggs and the blood of animals. They were being prepared to enter the dark and hidden places of good and evil spirits in order to both invoke and remove curses. Their new "calling" was to become a part of a secret brotherhood that has functioned in the Mayan world for thousands of years, a brotherhood that thrives in evil and darkness.

After the calling to receive the cross, the initiates were baptized in the river four times. It is noteworthy that as Christians, we are called upon to be baptized one time in the name of the Father, the Son and the Holy Spirit. Perhaps the Mayan priests added a dark being to their godhead. Their goal is to secure access to power wherever they can find it. For them, power is found in the blood of chickens and other animals — blood that has been drained from the beasts' veins and spilled upon the fires of sacrifice. It is truly a darkness where the light of Christ has never penetrated.

I wish I could tell you that the events described above were rare. The truth is, however, that these events are as old and as common among the Tajumulco Mam as the setting of the sun each day. In Ixchiguan, there are over a hundred *espiritistas*, *chimanes* and *brujos*. In Tajumulco there are even more. In Nuevo Porvenir, approximately one out of every two men is a practicing witch doctor! In the little village of El Triumfo, where we planted our last new church, there are at least 10 *chimanes*!

Is it any wonder that there is so much darkness in Tajumulco Mam country? Satan has had such a stronghold there for thousands of years, it's no surprise how bound and broken the people are.

One of our brethren, Rudy, took a walk awhile back to a sacrifice site only five minutes away from the Baptist church in Tajumulco and watched live sacrifices being carried out. One particular image remained burned into his brain. One *chiman* had slaughtered enough animals to fill a huge glass candleholder entirely with blood. As Rudy watched, the Mayan priest offered that blood to the spirits in order to accomplish the will of those who were paying him.

What does the cross mean to you? Do we realize that if it were not for the blood Jesus spilled for us on Calvary's cross that we would be wholly lost to the darkness of the Evil One? Our minds would be clouded and confused, veiled in darkness. Were it not for the cross of Christ, you and I would be no different from the Tajumulco Mam or any other pagan group anywhere else in the world. Without Christ we would also live in darkness, in fear with very little promise, doomed to place our best hopes in the blood of chickens and turkeys.

The cross may be a stumbling block to those who are perishing, but to those of us who are being saved, it truly is the power of God! Because of Jesus we are set free. Our sins are paid for by Jesus' blood. By Him we do not have to fear the spirit world and try to please the dark powers. In Jesus we already have a High Priest, one who mediates forevermore between us and a loving heavenly Father to accomplish our salvation and eternal relationship with Him. Can we grasp even a little of what that means?

As we go through our day-to-day activities, may we be reminded of how beautiful the cross is to those who believe in

Him. It may be an ugly instrument that the devil has used to torture and imprison untold millions in our world, but to us, it is a symbol of hope, of life-changing forgiveness, and of restoration from death to life. For too long the cross has been misunderstood. Today, let us tell the meaning of the cross to as many as we can. Tell it with boldness! Tell it with gladness, for the cross makes all the difference for us.

Because of the cross, our shame is taken away, our suffering becomes His suffering, and we trade our darkness for His light. Because of the cross, our bondage is broken, our eyes are opened, and hell becomes heaven. How amazing; how marvelous!

Will you receive the cross today?

# CHAPTER SEVEN

## Beginning Again

## 7.1

## To Dream Again

*After this, the word of the Lord came to Abram in a vision:*
*Do not be afraid, Abram. I am your shield, your very great reward.*
*But Abram said, "O Sovereign Lord, what can you give me*
*since I remain childless ...?"*

...

*He took him outside and said, "Look up at the heavens*
*and count the stars — if indeed you can count them."*
*Then he said to him, "So shall your offspring be."*
*– Genesis 15:1, 2a, 5*

DO YOU EVER FEEL OLD, tired and used up? (I hear some of you saying, "Most days!") Do you ever get caught up in thinking that your best days are already behind you? Many of us do feel this way from time to time. Life has a way of wearing us down, and we're not exactly the men and women we used to be.

A friend said to me awhile back that every time she looks into the mirror, an old, scary woman is there staring back at her! It is not a pretty sight to see ourselves aging. On especially bad days, we may fear we really don't have much left in us, that we are already over the hill, burned out and worn out. Am I right?

Someone said to me just the other day that he had become a lot more concerned with the hereafter these days. He said that nearly every time he enters a room of his house, he has to stop and ask himself, *What am I here after?*

Sometimes though, when we think that we are coming to an end, we are actually just beginning and simply don't know it yet.

When Abraham contemplated the Lord's work in his life, he probably felt that he had traveled a long way. As he left Ur, he left behind his home and most of his friends and family to set off on the adventure of a lifetime. Then later, as he stopped for a while in Haran, he must have felt that he had traveled far. His journey and adventures were amazing for a man of his time. Indeed, he lived a full life!

Abraham had a beautiful wife named Sarah, but as he entered his old age, he still did not have any children with her. This was a great disappointment for him. A son was the key to carrying on the lineage for a father. Also, what good were the gains of a man's life if he had no son to whom he could pass them on? This was the one sore point in a life that had been well lived.

When Abraham reached a ripe old age, he must have felt that he was pretty well washed up. God may have promised him a son, but when he looked into a mirror all he saw was an old man, and when he looked at his wife, he saw an old woman well past the age for bearing children. He had waited all those years for his last great dream to be fulfilled, and now it was too late! It is no wonder, then, that Abraham responded with frustration when the Lord reminded him of his "reward" and of the plans He had for making Abraham's future offspring into a great nation. "... What can you give me since I remain childless ... ?" Abraham asked the Lord (Gen. 15:2).

*Look, Lord,* Abraham may have thought. *The jig is up. I am now an old man, and my time is about over. Don't kid me, Lord.*

*I know the truth about this stage of my life. I am never going to have a son by Sarah, and You and I both know it. I'm too old! I've just got to accept the fact.*

It was at that point that the Lord taught Abraham a great lesson. Abraham was spending far too much time looking in the mirror and not nearly enough time looking up at the stars and dreaming! The Lord had instructed him, "Look up at the heavens and count the stars — if indeed you can count them. ... So shall your offspring be" (Gen. 15:5, NIV). It's as though the Lord were saying, *It's not over, Abraham. You might think it is, but it's not! And, you, my son, are far from finished. I have truly great plans for you, so just hang on!*

Did you know that Abraham was 100 years old when he saw the fulfillment of God's promise to him? He and Sarah must have taken a lot of kidding over starting to have children at their very advanced age because they named their son Isaac, which means "laughter." (Perhaps it was a real case of "he who laughs last, laughs best"?)

And the story doesn't end there! Abraham actually lived another 75 years, married again after Sarah died, fathered six more sons, endured further trials, won more victories, and established a heritage that was the beginning of the great nation of Israel! Not bad for the second wind of an old man, was it? Not bad at all! Once he stopped looking so much at the mirror and started looking up at the stars, he was able to get on with the rest of his life and with the excitement God still had in store for him!

May I share something? When I was a younger man, I had some big dreams for my life. I wanted to go to college and then on to seminary. I wanted to marry the woman of my dreams and have children. I wanted to become a minister and serve as a

160

pastor in the United States. Then I wanted to become a missionary and minister around the world telling others about Jesus. I wanted to earn a doctorate. I wanted to travel and devote my life to planting the gospel where it had never been sown before.

By the grace of God, all of these things have been accomplished! We have already had a wonderful ministry that has spanned three continents! (Please believe me, I say this not to boast but to give God the credit for it all!)

One day I was taking a moment to celebrate all the wonderful things that God had done in our lives, and I caught myself making the statement, *All of my dreams have already been accomplished — every single one!* I said this with a smile, but afterward, these words hung in my throat and settled in my stomach like a meal that didn't quite agree with me.

At first I didn't know what was wrong. As I reviewed my words and the accomplishments of my life, I thought, *I have loved my life ... every step of the way. I would not change any major decision that I have ever made! My life has been absolutely great! So what's the problem?*

Somewhere inside, a voice confirmed, *Yes, your life has been great. It has been a dream come true for you! But what comes next, Gary? Or have you stopped dreaming?*

Somewhere along the way I had indeed stopped dreaming. That realization shook me, and over a period of time I have allowed myself to begin to dream new dreams again. As I have begun to dare to look up at the heavens and to see the stars overhead, I have begun to feel less like an old man and a burned-out, tired old missionary. Once again I'm asking myself, *What else does God have for me to accomplish?*

I'm convinced that too many people have stopped dreaming! They have accepted their victories and defeats from the past and have settled into a holding pattern, thinking that their best days are behind them. Are you one of them? If so, I believe that God is saying to us, "It is time to dream again!" It's time to get up and to plan for part two, part three, or part four of our lives. There is still far to go and so much that He wants to do through us! Look up! For He is the God of the future, not merely the God of the past and the present!

If you are looking in the mirror and thinking that it is about over for you, you might do well to rethink your status! What does God have for you to do in this period of your life, and where do you feel God's pleasure? Focus on those areas and get on with it! After all, Abraham was 100 years old before he connected with the rest of his life — all 75 years of it! What makes you think you're through yet?

Lift up your head and see the stars God has placed ahead of you and get started dreaming new dreams in Him!

## 7.2
### A Seat Not Taken

*Since then we have a great high priest who has passed*
*through the heavens, Jesus, the Son of God, let us hold fast*
*our confession. For we have not a high priest who is unable to*
*sympathize with our weaknesses, but one who in every respect*
*has been tempted as we are, yet without sin.*
*Let us then with confidence draw near to the throne of grace,*
*that we may receive mercy and find grace to help in time of need.*
*– Hebrews 4:14–16*

PEOPLE CAN BE CRUEL. Why do we hurt others? Even apart
from true sadists, the rest of us inflict pain on others many times
without even thinking about it. Perhaps cruelty on the part of
human beings is natural and should be expected. Maybe cruelty
is just the result of our thinking of ourselves first, so much so
that we forget to ask ourselves what would work best for others.
Or is it that we just don't care most of the time? We are all so
busy with our "us-ness" that we can't seem to get beyond it.

Do you remember the scene in the movie "Forrest Gump"
where little Forrest gets on the school bus for the first time? He
doesn't know anyone, and as he makes his way down the aisle
with funny-looking braces on his legs, the other kids stare at
him. Each time he spots an empty seat, the kid next to it says,
"Can't sit here! This seat's taken!" As Forrest moves farther and

farther toward the back of the bus, not many seats are left. Even so, he continues to hear, "Can't! ... Taken!"

Many of us can relate to the character of Forrest Gump because we also suffered at the hands of others when we were children. Maybe we were fatter than the other kids. Maybe our clothes were not as nice as others' or maybe we were not as good looking. Perhaps we were not as good at sports and were not chosen for games until the very end when there was no one else to choose from.

For a hundred and one reasons, we knew what it was like to be made fun of, left out or treated badly by the other children. And we have spent a lifetime trying to forget those experiences, even though deep down inside, we know those scars will never go away while we live upon this Earth.

Wounds like these cause many people to feel unloved, undervalued and unworthy. Their self-esteem suffers — not only throughout childhood but into adulthood.

Several years ago, I attended a conference with a large gathering of other Christian leaders. Everyone there was in Christian service, and although I didn't know many people, it was supposed to be like family. On the first morning, we all gathered for breakfast in the hotel restaurant. I served myself from the buffet, and then looked around for someone I knew to sit with. Not spotting anyone, I decided to be sociable anyway and walked over to a table of men where there was an empty chair. I introduced myself and asked if I could join them for breakfast.

One of the men quickly put his hand over the empty place at the table and told me someone else might be joining them later, so there was no room at the table for me. I nodded, took my plate and sat down at another table across the room. As I did, I made myself a promise. I told myself that for the rest of my life, I would see to it that there would always be room at my table for anyone who asked to sit down!

Some of you reading this have been hurt when you have been denied a seat at the table, so to speak. Maybe someone has treated you badly. Perhaps a spouse has been unfaithful to you or a child of yours acts as if he's ashamed of you. Has a close friend let you down? Maybe you have been passed over for a promotion. Or can it be that you are simply ignored and that others don't care enough to find out who you really are? Whatever the cause, you too have heard a voice that said, "You can't sit here!" And it hurts.

The Book of Hebrews tells us that if we are in Christ, we are not facing our hurts or fighting our battles alone. We have One in heaven who is standing in the presence of God Almighty serving as our High Priest and making intercession for us. His name is Jesus. You see, He can sympathize with our hurts because He too has been hurt. He knows what it's like to be rejected, despised and denied a seat at the table of humanity. And because of all He has suffered, He now stands at the throne of God so that we might receive mercy and grace ... and help in all our times of need.

I believe that in heaven there is a seat not taken. It is not taken yet because it has been reserved and kept especially for you because you are in Christ Jesus! You see, I believe that God is somewhat like the character Jenny in "Forrest Gump," who said to Forrest what the Father is saying to each of us: *You can sit here if you want.* Not only is He willing for us to sit with Him, He has actually written our names down and saved our place. And as long as Jesus stands as your intercessor, regardless of your past sins, hurts and scars, no one can ever say to you that the seat is taken! It is your seat... with your name on it... and it has been placed alongside a host of others from throughout time who also have been redeemed by the Lamb. These companions, unlike those we have encountered on Earth, are eagerly looking forward to the day when you come and take your place!

The words from the old Irish hymn "Before the Throne of God Above" say it well:

> *Before the throne of God above,*
> *I have a strong, a perfect plea,*
> *A great High Priest whose name is "Love,"*
> *Who ever lives and pleads for me.*
> *My name is graven on His hands,*
> *My name is written on His heart;*
> *I know that while in heav'n He stands*
> *no tongue can bid me thence depart.*
> *No tongue can bid me thence depart.*

Yes, this world can be a cruel place where we are hurt and scarred. But if ever you feel that you can't find a place to sit, be assured that somewhere in a place not so very far away there is a seat not taken, one that is being reserved just for you. I know this because it is my Father's place, and He is waiting for you to one day take your seat there. And when you do, all the hurts and sorrows of this life will finally be forgotten.

Only joy at being in the presence of Jesus will remain!

## 7.3
## Unfailing Love

*But I have trusted in thy steadfast love;*
*my heart shall rejoice in thy salvation.*
– Psalm 13:5

THE WORD "LOVE" gets a lot of use these days. People say it all the time and mean very different things. For instance, one person will say, "I just love your new clothes!" Another will say, "Oh, I just love that new grilled chicken platter that they have." Movie stars will often say, "We're in love forever!" Then, the next thing the public hears is that the couple has filed for divorce — that is, if they ever bothered to get married in the first place.

Is it any wonder that the divorce rate in the United States hovers above 50 percent among Christians and non-Christians alike? We, in our fallen, broken society, don't even know what the word "love" means!

The Tajumulco Mam people of Guatemala don't really even have a word for "love." They usually use the word for "want." I want food. I want land. I want a wife. It is all the same. Perhaps this is more honest, considering the short-term meaning that we ascribe to the word "love." If you don't understand what love is, one word is as good as another.

Who among us does not desire down deep in his or her heart to really know love? It is a universal hunger. We don't know how to go about finding the real thing, so we accept some substitute and just call it "love."

Yet we struggle and search for the real thing as we go through our lives. We yearn to love and be loved. Why, then, is it so illusive? Can it be that most of us don't understand love because we haven't really been able to grasp God's love for us? Can it be that we are so flawed by the kind of love we've been shown that we just don't get it? We display imperfect love to each other because we are scarred individuals where love is concerned. Human models are often just not good enough. We need nothing less than a supernatural encounter with the love of God.

The story that I am about to share with you deeply touched my heart. It is a true story, although I have changed a couple of the details in order to protect the identity of the person involved. To me, it is a reminder that God deeply loves each one of us and that if we will put our trust in Him, we can learn how to love God, each other and even ourselves. This is a story of God's unfailing love. ...

During the 1940s, Michael was one of seven children born into a Christian family. Although his parents took him to church and tried their best to raise him right, he didn't feel loved. He heard all the right language but never experienced love's grip upon his life. As he grew, he became involved in destructive activities such as street racing and using drugs.

One day after using cocaine, Michael became tense and paranoid and thought he saw a demonic shape in the corner of the room. The eyes of the figure seemed to glow brighter and brighter as they stared right at him. Suddenly the shape turned its head toward him and said three terrifying words: "You are mine!" This nearly scared Michael to death! He frantically wondered if the experience might be real and began to call out to God for help.

*This can't be happening!* he pleaded to God. *Help me!*

The next day, Michael was due to report for military service in a northern state. Still tortured by his experience of the night before, he was in a terrible state of mind as he drove down the interstate toward the Army base. The more he drove, the more upset he became. It was as if the emptiness of his whole life was catching up with him. He became convinced that no one in the world cared for him. He was unloved and all alone with no protection from his own horrible sins or from even Satan himself. In despair he repeated over and over, *Oh God! Help me!*

Then, out of nowhere, a billboard came into view. It was one of dozens of billboards, but for some reason it was the one Michael noticed. It had only three words written in large letters: "Jesus loves you!" Although at another time in his life he probably would have scoffed at the billboard's triteness, at that moment he felt strangely that God was answering his prayer and telling him that in spite of all his circumstances, He still loved him. He was so moved that he pulled his car over and began to sob. The tears flowed and just would not stop. It was at that moment that Michael began to believe in the love of God through Jesus Christ.

When Michael arrived at the Army base, he checked his papers and reported to the proper barracks. There was no one else there at the time, so he chose an empty bunk and put his gear down. He then took out the Bible that he had stuck in his sack for boot camp. He opened it up and began to read with a new hunger to understand what Jesus had done for him. Some time went by, and while he was deep in his reading, the sergeant came in and noticed what he was doing.

"Soldier, what are you doing here?!" he yelled.

Michael jumped up, put his Bible down, and quickly handed over his papers. "I am reporting for duty, sir!" he said.

After examining the papers, the sergeant then glared at the Bible Michael had been reading. With an angry look, he asked, "Is that a Bible that you're reading there, soldier?"

"Yes sir, it is," Michael responded.

"Soldier, are you going to tell me that you are a Christian?"

Here it is, Michael thought. The moment of truth. A spark of belief had flickered to life inside him as he sat sobbing underneath the billboard, but he had not yet spoken of his belief to a living soul. A second or two ticked by as Michael prepared himself for the persecution that would surely follow if he answered "yes." Somehow, though, he found the courage to look the sergeant in the eye and say, "Yes sir, I am a Christian!"

As he braced himself, the sergeant began to smile. "You know what?" he said. "I'm a Christian, too!" He left the barracks encouraging Michael to "just keep on reading that Bible!"

From time to time throughout boot camp, the sergeant would talk to him about his faith in the Lord. Once, in the middle of artillery exercises, the sergeant came over to him and asked him privately if he had his pocket Bible on him. He did. With the other men watching, the sergeant gruffly told Michael to follow him and led him away from the others, over a couple of hills and into the shade of a large tree.

"Michael, why don't you just sit right down there and use this time to study your Bible?" he said. "I'll be back for you later."

So all afternoon Michael stretched out in the shade and read the New Testament. The sergeant's concern for him was not lost on Michael.

Today Michael knows what real love is. He has been a missionary in Guatemala for many years now and has made it his life's goal to show others the love of Jesus. He fondly remembers his old drill sergeant, his brother in Christ, and his mentor in learning how to help others to grow into their new selves through faith.

I would wish the same type of experience for you today. May God place unmistakable signs of His great love in your life — a love that is for all circumstances, a love that penetrates your soul, a love that is unfailing. Beyond that, I would wish that you and I could be like that drill sergeant and help others to understand for the first time in their lives how much God really loves them.

After all, that's why we're here.

## 7.4
## No Place for the Poor

*And while they were there, the time came for her to be delivered.*
*And she gave birth to her first-born son and wrapped him*
*in swaddling cloths, and laid him in a manger,*
*because there was no place for them in the inn.*
– Luke 2:6–7

CHILDREN AREN'T ALLOWED to choose where they're born. They arrive wherever their mother happens to be when the time comes. But most of the time parents do get to choose the place. If you already have children, what kind of place did you choose for your child's birth? I'm sure you chose the best hospital, birthing center or home available. We all want the very best for our children.

I know that when our first child, Lindsay, was due, we chose the Audubon Hospital in Louisville, Kentucky. It was a wonderful hospital and was the site where the Jarvik 7 artificial heart was implanted in a patient in 1984, about the same period as Lindsay's birth. It was a top-of-the-line hospital in several areas and was the best hospital we could find during our seminary days there in Louisville. We also had the best doctor we could find to deliver our first baby. Nothing but the best for our child!

Go back to Christmas 1979 with me for a moment. We were serving as missionary journeymen in the eastern jungles of Ecuador, and we lived right on the Aguarico River. Lily ran a prenatal and postpartal clinic from our house, and she frequently had ladies in for checkups. She would get them connected with a doctor in the town of Lago Agrio and help them through the birth process.

On that Christmas Day the clinic was closed. We had been invited to spend the day with another missionary family in Lago Agrio, Garreth and Elaine Joiner. After we had opened our few presents in our little home, we headed up the road to be with the Joiners, looking forward to a wonderful Christmas dinner together. We had it, too, with all the trimmings … a Christmas celebration fit for a king!

When we got back home, we discovered that we had company. A woman who was heavy into labor had traveled for hours, crossing a river and riding a horse for miles in order to get to our house. Upon arriving, she found our clinic closed and the place locked up tight, but she was exhausted and could travel no farther.

With no other option, she gave birth to her first child there in the dirt, on the ground in front of our house. She was fully exposed to the hot sun, the passers-by, and to the ever-present jungle insects. Instead of a sanitary hospital bed with fresh linens and an expert team of doctors and nurses to attend her and her little baby, she had only her husband to make her as comfortable as possible there on the ground. She delivered a son that day. She welcomed him to our world with all the love and care that she could provide, even though her bed was only some smooth dirt.

Go back even further with me … to the first Christmas. Mary rode a donkey, and she and Joseph were also traveling miles. When they arrived at the best inn that they could find, they found it closed up tight. The best they could do was to find a clean place in the straw within a barn for Mary to give birth to her baby. After He was born, the best that she could find to lay Him in was a manger — a food trough for the animals to eat from. How could it be that the God of all creation — the God of eternity who owns everything — allowed His Son Jesus to be born in such a primitive, dirty setting? Why did He not choose a more suitable time and place for the King of kings and the Lord of lords to be born? How could an animal trough in a Bethlehem barn be the chosen place?

I think that God in His infinite wisdom chose to allow His only Son to be born the way He was for a reason. While we might seek cleanliness, comfort and acceptable accom-modations, He sought to connect with the poorest of the day. He allowed His Son to be born in the same way the majority of other poor children are born. God cared not for luxury or comfort. He cared only for those lost and broken, and He cared enough to want His Son to know their suffering and their great need.

No, God is not like us in His planning. He is more like the woman who gave birth in front of Lily's clinic. You see, He cares deeply for us — for all of us, not merely the privileged or those who "have it all together." He cares for ordinary people, poor people, broken people like us — sinners who have no one but Him to go to for help.

This is the message of God's great love for us: In order to lift us out of our spiritual poverty and suffering, God meets us where we are and as we are. His plan is to accomplish nothing less than to change our lives forever, no matter where we started. He went to the heart of our commonness, our dirtiness, and our desperate poverty and invested His very best in us. How can we do less than to invest ourselves in His purpose of redemption for the lost world all around us? Only then can we really be able to understand what God's love is all about.

Spent any time with poor people in barns lately? God has.

## 7.5
## Dog on a Roof
🍂

*His watchmen are blind, they are all without knowledge;*
*they are all dumb dogs, they cannot bark;*
*dreaming, lying down, loving to slumber.*
– Isaiah 56:10

*"... [A]nd you will know the truth, and the truth will make you free."*
*They answered him, "We are descendants of Abraham,*
*and have never been in bondage to any one.*
*How is it that you say, 'You will be made free'?"*
– John 8:32–33

ONE OF THE THINGS that all of us have in common is our desire to be free. No matter where we live or what the conditions of our lives are, we all want to be able to make our own decisions and live our own lives. We want to be able to think for ourselves and to express ourselves as we so choose. To be free to sleep out under the stars if we wish, watch the sun come up over a lake, and see the early morning mist rise up out of the waters. These are experiences beyond price.

To be free is the desire hidden deep within every heart. What is heartbreaking, though, is that so many people are not free. Because of oppressive governments, many nations are not free. Because of the consequences of our past decisions, many people are not free. Many souls are locked in the darkness of imprisonment. Sometimes our conditions are easily apparent, and our prison bars are seen by all. At other times, though, our chains are not readily visible because our bondage is on the inside — in our hearts and minds.

I am very much aware that some of you who read these words may be incarcerated in prison. The hours and the days of waiting and hoping to be free may seem endless. The routine of each new day is much like the one before it and pretty much the same as it will be tomorrow. I can't pretend to really understand what it must be like, but I know some days it must seem unbearable. I can only wish from a distance that you might one day be truly free and that you may have a second chance at living in the bright sunshine again. My advice to you is: Don't give up hope! I believe with all my heart that God's light can shine brightly in the darkest room. Freedom begins in the soul of a man — even in a dark prison cell — if he accepts God's way through Jesus Christ. Never, ever give up hope!

Prisons are not the only places where people aren't free. Often the most tragic cases are those that most people don't recognize. I have come to believe that many churches also contain countless individuals who are not really free. Oh, in our churches we sing, read and talk about freedom a whole lot. But talking about freedom and living it are two different matters. Perhaps the worst tragedy of all is that so many people are not free — and they don't even realize it!

Our neighbors once kept a guard dog on the roof of their house. His name was Terry, and he was a huge, black Rottweiler with fierce-looking teeth. Every day Terry would be left on top of the family's cement roof to watch over the front entry to their house. He would run back and forth and slobber on many who walked by the gate that led into their business. He appeared very vicious, and he frightened many as they walked by. Terry was loose and on the prowl, many assumed.

We, however, knew better, for Terry could not get down from their roof. He was stuck up there day in and day out by those who owned him. Although he could bark, he could not bite, for he was imprisoned on the roof, away from the rest of the world that walked on the ground. Because he was locked on the roof, Terry spent much of his time just observing the world around him instead of participating in it. He was just a dog on the roof.

Eventually, Terry passed away. He no longer runs back and forth across the cement roof, and he no longer barks at those who walk free on the outside. The sound of his bark is now silent, and its influence on the people who walk below his roof every day is largely forgotten.

I sometimes wonder if the church as an institution has settled for being just a "Terry." Have we preached separation from sin for so long that we have begun to believe that we should be separated from sinners? Have we somehow convinced ourselves that God's will for us is that we should stand back like a dog on a roof, separated from the world below us, barking at those walking by on the ground below? If so, then we have gotten it wrong. So terribly wrong.

Why do we treat the church like a palace that needs to be defended? Surely God's purpose for His church is more than just defense!

Jesus taught His disciples to go out into the streets and to involve themselves with the poor, the hurting and the lost. To make a real difference. He did not want the primary function of his disciples to be guarding a palace! Instead, He sent His kingdom builders out into the midst of sinners who needed to hear the truth and be set free. The problem is that too many Christians prefer to stay on the roof and guard the palace instead of putting God's will into effect on the sidewalks below where the people pass by each day.

Someone once said that the kingdom is built in the streets by those who are willing to leave the palace. I believe that only when the church hits the streets in loving service are its members truly set free! Free to live, free to love, free to serve, and free to get involved with the sinful humanity below it for whom Jesus died. Until the testimony of what Jesus has done in our lives through His love and grace flows freely through us into our communities, the lost will give the church no more attention than they would a dog on a roof!

Can you imagine the effect on our world if more Christians spent much more time in the streets (like Jesus did!) actually loving people (instead of just condemning them) and being salt to the unsavory and light to the people who live in the midst of the darkness? While there may be some benefit to barking at passers-by who are doing things we don't approve of, there is so much more that can be done if the church is unleashed into the world!

Jesus said that we would know the truth and that the truth would set us free. My prayer is that this would be so in our lives — that we would learn to live life unleashed by His love and empowered by His grace to serve.

Sure beats merely being dogs on a roof, wouldn't you say?

## CHAPTER EIGHT

## Experiencing Thanksgiving

## 8.1
## Learning To Be Thankful

*Praise the Lord! O give thanks to the Lord, for he is good;*
*his steadfast love endures for ever! Who can utter*
*the mighty doings of the Lord, or show forth all his praise?*
– Psalms 106:1–2

As a community of Christians, we share a commonality in the goodness of God and in our salvation through Jesus Christ. After that, we begin to separate in what we enjoy and in what matters most to us. We like different things, and we are made glad by different circumstances. What are some of the things on your list that make you glad today?

Call me strange, but Thanksgiving is one of the things on my list. Of all the holiday seasons, it is my personal favorite. It's a simple time (at least in our family) when only two things are really important: (1) Pausing to remember how blessed we are and how much the Lord has done for us, and (2) celebrating God's goodness in giving us family and friends and spending unhindered time with them. It is all so honest and uncomplicated. There are no lists of must-buy presents, no season of perpetual meetings and parties to get through, and no "killer" schedule of travel, activities and programs. It is just stopping for a brief day or two and remembering what is important in our lives. My soul is always fed during the Thanksgiving season. Pausing, remembering and celebrating God's goodness is too seldom done. We go and go, and we do and do, but how often do we pause and just give thanks for what He has done?

Two short tales from my family's experience long ago encourage me to be thankful. They both go back to the time of the Depression when my mother's family lived on a farm in rural South Carolina. Although things were hard all over, they usually had salted beef or pork in a box on the porch, cattle in the pasture that gave them milk and beef, chickens all over that provided them with eggs and a Sunday dinner whenever needed, and crops galore during most of the year. For the winter months they ate all the foods that they had cured, canned or put away during the summer. They all worked hard, but they also lived well.

Not everyone was so fortunate. Throughout her childhood, my mother, Mary Stone, witnessed a stream of people who showed up on their farm asking for help. Most of them were looking for a little food and some decent work. My grandfather, Dan Patton, had no money to pay them, but he could offer them meals at his table and a place to sleep in the barn in exchange for helping on the farm. Some of them would stay a few days and others would stay a few weeks.

One of them became a regular guest on their farm. His name was Johnny Plunder. We never learned where Johnny was from exactly, but for several years he would show up and move into the barn for a few weeks at a time. Johnny may have been taking a vacation from his regular life, for it seemed that he genuinely liked being there with my grandfather and working on his farm in exchange for room and board. I have often wondered about his life, given that he seemed so thankful to live in a barn and to work for food for a matter of weeks several years in a row. How could it be that living with animals in a barn and eating all your meals with a family not your own was better than the other circumstances of Johnny's life? It all comes down to asking one simple question: Compared to what? Compared to his other options, Johnny Plunder apparently felt glad to have decent work, food and a place in the barn to sleep.

During this same period, my mother and her brothers and sisters walked to school every school day. During warm weather, the half-mile or so walk was not too bad. In winter, however, it was harder. They didn't have the money to buy new shoes every year, and they quickly learned how to put cardboard in their soles to plug holes, and they learned how to tie up the torn places with wire so that their shoes would hold together enough to keep out the cold and wet. Every other kid in the community did pretty much the same thing, so no one thought much about it — except for one particular family.

One little girl in my mother's class had no shoes at all. On cold days her little feet would be nearly frozen by the time she got to school. At the schoolhouse was an old coal stove that had to be started each day. It would take awhile for the room to warm up, and when the little girl's feet started to warm back up, she would cry because of the pain. My mother remembers her teacher taking the little girl into her lap and rubbing her feet to help the feeling to come back in them.

What does all this have to do with being thankful? Just this: All of us, no matter the circumstances of our lives, have something for which we can be thankful. We can choose to focus on the things that we wish were different (e.g., sleeping in a barn, wearing old, torn shoes, or having no shoes and feeling the pain of frozen feet), or we can focus on the good things that make our lives better (such as having warm, clean hay to sleep on, having strong pieces of cardboard and wire with which shoes can be fixed, or having a loving, caring teacher who would hold you in her lap and soothe your pain by gently massaging your feet).

While few of us today have to endure such drastic circumstances, all of us wish some part of our life's burdens were different. However, sometimes we cannot change our circumstances, and the problems will not just go away. We can change only so much, and the rest we just have to accept. In times of angst or frustration, we would benefit by asking ourselves how our situation matches up with other alternatives. … Compared to what?

Would you join me in trying to look beyond the inconveniences of life to see the hand of God at work during even the most difficult times? He has promised to always be with us and to never forsake us. When we suffer, He takes us on His lap and massages our spirits until we again feel the warmth of His love.

If we really think about it, we are so blessed by the Lord. Most of us live charmed lives, thanks to the grace of God. We have so many blessings, and, compared to so many others in our world today, we have nothing to complain about — only to be grateful for.

I won't wait for Thanksgiving to remember Johnny Plunder and the little friend of my mother's with her cold feet in the lap of a caring teacher. And none of us need wait to remember

God's goodness to us all and give thanks to Him for His blessings in our lives. After all, we can never express enough thanks for "the mighty doings" of the Lord!

We can only be grateful.

## 8.2
### Congregating at the Lavatory:
### A Thanksgiving Meditation on the Simple Things

*He who has a bountiful eye will be blessed,*
*for he shares his bread with the poor.*
— Proverbs 22:9

*Enter his gates with thanksgiving, and his courts with praise!*
*Give thanks to him, bless his name! For the Lord is good;*
*his steadfast love endures for ever,*
*and his faithfulness to all generations.*
— Psalm 100:4–5

THANKSGIVING IS A TIME for taking inventory, a time for noticing all the blessings in our lives and for giving thanks to almighty God. We ought to be doing it every day, but at least we can pause during this special season of the year and remember the rich blessings of God.

What are you most thankful for? I think we all would agree on some obvious things, including: God's grace and forgiveness, our family and friends, our health, meaningful work and the provision of God in our daily lives. Now I would like to offer some not-so-common thoughts on how to express our gratitude.

On a flight that was returning us to our missions work overseas, we were seated in a wide-body 747 Delta jet when the cabin attendant started the usual spiel about safety regulations, including how to buckle your seatbelt. (Not that I'm complaining, mind you, but we have all heard the instructions so many times that most of us could give the speech ourselves.) However, after the basic instructions were complete, the flight attendant said something I had never heard before.

"Do not," she said, "congregate at the lavatories! If you do, we will have to disperse you."

I couldn't help but smile. I have never heard of anything so ridiculous! I suppose they must have had problems with too many people blocking the aisles while waiting to use the lavatories.

The ridiculousness of it all started me to thinking, though, about how things would be if there were no lavatories on airplanes or in our homes. It may sound simple to you, but I would cast my vote any day for the indoor flush toilet as perhaps the most useful invention of our time! Indoor plumbing is just another example of the many blessings we in the West take for granted every single day. Oh sure, electricity, the telephone, television, computers, cars, planes, etc. are wonderful. But where would we be without the convenience of flush toilets and indoor plumbing in our homes and in planes and buses? What if there were no lavatories to congregate around?

In times of need, the simple things of life can make us glad. Too many times we complain about what we don't have rather than giving thanks for those we do. If we really think about it, my guess is that the great majority of us have always had everything we have ever really needed!

Lily and I lived in the jungles of Ecuador for a while without indoor plumbing and electricity. I can assure you that a person can live just fine with candles and with blocks of ice to keep food from spoiling. It's not as hard as you might think to live without all the modern appliances. You don't really need television if you can see the stars at night. You don't have to have the computer if you can still read books and magazines and if you can write letters to friends and family. And life without a telephone may actually be a blessing! But take away indoor plumbing, and life becomes harsh and boorish. When is the last time we gave thanks to God for the simple things that give our lives grace and dignity?

Perhaps our most memorable Thanksgiving was in Lago Agrio, Ecuador in 1980. We lived along the banks of the Aguarico River. We joined in with friends who came out from the city and friends from the Peace Corps who lived farther in the jungle, and we all celebrated together without the conveniences of modern life. We came together from all over, much as the Pilgrims and the Indians did for the first Thanksgiving. We killed our own turkey and chickens, baked cakes in a Dutch oven on top of our little stove, and prepared everything from scratch. And we had a blast!

It was so much fun and so full of simplicity ... just realizing how grateful we were to be alive and to have the presence of the Lord with us as well as meaningful relationships with cherished friends. So many people seek the wealth and conveniences of life, all the while forgetting that it is the simple things that money can't buy that really make life rich. At times like these, Lily and I realize how extraordinarily rich we genuinely are.

While we are thinking about simplicity, I would like to suggest some simple things that might help restore some of the meaning of Thanksgiving. Forgive me if I seem overly simplistic, but sometimes the obvious can escape us if we're not careful.

How about the art of storytelling? When is the last time you sat with your family and laughed as you told stories about times past? (Does your fireplace work? If so, why not fire it up and stop worrying about the little bit of soot and the smoke that will only make your home look lived in anyway?) Spending time together is almost a lost art in many families. If you haven't used this gift in a while, why not try it during the holidays?

What about sharing around the table the things in your life that you are thankful for? Our children sometimes remind us of the simple things that make them glad. Too often we only think of the more obvious things.

Have you considered a Thanksgiving offering to the poor? Find some person or agency that you can make a difference in by giving an offering. We forget sometimes just how much a blessing giving to others really is!

On a more radical note, some of our friends have considered reducing the amount of money that they need each month to live on. Some are even considering selling their home and moving into a smaller place so that they might invest their monies in the things that they believe in most. This is not for everyone, but it is something to at least ask ourselves about.

Get your family to make a list of the things in their lives that are not that important and compare them with the things that are most important. Share your lists with one another. You might find some surprises. Make time for those you love, and gather them around you in your home. Tell them how much they mean to you. Then show them — even if you have to drop some other activities to make it happen.

Slow down and spend time with God! Yes, it is hard to do, and, yes, there are a million other things we could be doing. But ask yourself: *Is there anything that is more important?*

My challenge to all of us is to slow down and take inventory of the many blessings of God in our lives. Whether you're thankful for indoor plumbing on airplanes (as your slightly crazed missionary friend is) or for the smile on your little girl's face as she says, "I love you, Mommy!" just before she falls asleep, thank God for His goodness to us in the simple things of life! The problems of our world and of our lifestyles can seem so complicated at times.

Why not seek to balance our lives by taking stock of and giving thanks for the basic, little things that give our lives real meaning?

## 8.3
## Thankfulness for the Times We Are Carried

*And they came, bringing to [Jesus] a paralytic*
*carried by four men. And when they could not get near him*
*because of the crowd, they removed the roof above him;*
*and when they had made an opening, they let down the pallet*
*on which the paralytic lay.*
– Mark 2:3–4

ONCE UPON A TIME, a fellow Mam missionary named Keith
Stamps journeyed to a place called Bullaj in Guatemala along
the Mexican border. He and a group of brothers from Sibinal
had been there trying to share the gospel and to plant a new
work. Getting to Bullaj was quite a hike and involved going
down about 4,000 feet over rocky and winding paths.

Keith and the Sibinal brothers spent several hours there
sharing their faith. After having visited the people of the village
and leading a worship service there, Keith and the brothers
started the arduous uphill trek out. In the process, Keith got sick.
He felt awful and became weaker and weaker.

It's not easy to climb 4,000 feet of rocks and slippery sand
when you're sick to your stomach. He tried to be strong, but the
hours of hiking began to take their toll. His body was spent. The
brothers, seeking to strengthen him, offered him some of their
raw eggs. What that gesture actually did was to give him more
nausea. Keith could hardly go on.

Then something unusual happened. One of the brothers from Sibinal was partially crippled and yet had made the trip without complaining. He had one good leg and one leg that did not work very well. Despite his infirmity, when he saw that Keith could hardly walk, he did not hesitate to offer to carry him on his back up the mountain. His offer was sincere. Instead of asking to be carried himself, he was offering to carry someone else up the rocky cliffs. Although Keith knew he couldn't let the struggling brother carry him all the way back up the mountain, his heart was touched.

I think back in my own experience to times when I was too weak to walk and many brothers carried me. Some of them had their own "crippled legs," and yet they felt enough of God's strength to support me. After all, we are all crippled in one way or another as we strive to climb the mountain. The difference is that some of us get so preoccupied with our own struggles that we never think about offering to carry anyone else. Thank God for those who, like the four friends in the Book of Mark who carried their lame friend to Jesus, forget their own weaknesses and concentrate on helping others. May we be more like them in our daily walk up the mountain.

How are your legs today?

## 8.4
## An African Tale

*"Today, when you hear his voice, do not harden your hearts*
*as in the rebellion, on the day of testing in the wilderness...."*
– Hebrews 3:7b–8

---

*...[F]or I have learned, in whatever state I am, to be content.*
*I know how to be abased, and I know how to abound;*
*in any and all circumstances I have learned*
*the secret of facing plenty and hunger, abundance and want.*
*I can do all things in him who strengthens me.*
– Philippians 4:11–13

A WISE MAN ONCE SAID that life is not a sprint — it is a marathon. How true that is! How fast we run for the first hundred yards dulls in comparison to how we do in the long haul and how we finish the race. When all is said and done, life is about surviving, staying in the race and not giving up.

How do we handle it when we are faced with terrible trials in the wildernesses of our journey? Some throw in the towel and give up when their walk with the Lord requires them to endure hardships they hadn't bargained for. Others confront their challenges one by one and do not give up until the journey is complete. We have much to learn from this second group of travelers.

What I am about to share with you is an amazing true story that proves that with God's help we can survive almost anything. It is the story of a 10-year-old boy named John who was living in Casablanca, Morocco with his parents. His father was connected to the military and was involved in training French soldiers there. His mother was a devout Christian lady who happened to be a close friend of C.S. Lewis.

One day when John was walking back to the apartment where they were staying, he saw his father's car parked on the street. John and his mother had only recently arrived in Casablanca and were waiting for his father. As John walked toward his apartment, suddenly fighting broke out all around him. Cars and buildings were blown to smithereens. He threw himself into a ditch and stayed there until the fighting ended.

When it was all over, everything around him was blown to bits — including the apartment building where he and his parents had been staying. Searching the rubble for his parents, he became more and more desperate as he realized that no one in the building could have survived the blasts.

John walked around in a daze, coming to grips with the surety that his parents were dead and that he was all alone. He didn't know what to do. He knew of no living relatives in Africa ... except for a lady whom he knew as "Aunt," but she lived all the way on the other side of the continent in Durban, South Africa! How could he possibly cross a continent so large and find her?

Not knowing what else to do, the 10-year-old took off north while he tried to figure things out. Where do you go when you know no one, and what do you do when you have nothing but the clothes on your back? After wandering the northern part of Africa for a while, he realized that the only thing to do was to go and find his aunt in Durban. Thus, alone and with no money or anyone to guide him, he began a more than 5,000-mile journey across one of the most dangerous continents on the Earth.

The complete story of John's survival and of his trek across Africa can only be fully told by John himself, but it has to be one of the most incredible stories ever. Allow me to share only a few highlights: During the 18 months it took John to cross the entire continent of Africa, he often journeyed alone but sometimes ran into others who allowed him to travel with them.

At various times he was taken in by hobos, ne'er-do-wells, British soldiers and others. Some experiences were horrible, such as the days he spent literally tied to a man with burned eyes who forced John to be his guide until he could see again. Other experiences were amazingly good! While traveling with some British soldiers, he was twice taken to meet with a writer named Ernest Hemingway who was visiting in Africa. Hemingway later apparently shared his stories about John with some other writers. Later on, a movie starring Edward G. Robinson was made called "A Boy Ten Feet Tall," which possibly was based on the original story of John's experience.

After 18 incredible months, John finally arrived in Durban, South Africa. He found his aunt, only to discover that she was not really his aunt but a dear friend of his mother's. Not only that, but after all that time, he finally learned that his parents had not been killed in the explosions. They had been in another apartment complex just down the road during the attack. They were alive and looking for him, though they feared him dead!

After John was reunited with his parents, he went on to lead an incredible life. Now married, he has a wonderful family and lives in Quetzaltenango, Guatemala. He is a Christian and serves God today with his life and many talents. He has his own business and also serves in at least two missionary capacities in the Xela area.

All that he has been through has molded him and made him both real — and real tough. After what he has lived through, John knows that anything is possible with God's help. Maybe one day he will write the full story of his life in book form as the few of us who know the truth about him have urged him to. (I have purposefully not mentioned his last name to protect his privacy.)

How would you like to travel 5,000 miles across Africa as a 10-year-old? How would you fare if you believed you were all alone in a strange land? John endured his incredible wilderness experience with courage, dignity and determination. Thank the Lord that you and I do not have to face what he lived through. Instead, we face other trials and walk through other "wildernesses," don't we?

At times we may live and make our decisions as though we are all alone in this world, but the truth is that our Father is still very much alive, and He will never abandon us on the journey. Through trials, struggles, dangers and hard times, even through hunger and famine, He has promised to see us to our journey's end if we will but let Him.

Though the journey may seem long and the way hard, don't give up until you see your walk completed. Awaiting at the end is good news and great joy! Whatever God is calling you to do today, do it! Don't stop or turn away when the trek gets hard or seems impossibly long.

Whether our wilderness adventure involves crossing Africa or staying put in our own hometown, we need to keep on until

our odyssey is ended. Go on ... you can make it with His help.
Don't stop or turn back.

John would tell you to keep the faith!

## 8.5
## A Gypsy Gospel
🍂

*Have this mind among yourselves, which is yours in Christ Jesus*
*who, though he was in the form of God, did not count equality*
*with God a thing to be grasped, but emptied himself,*
*taking the form of a servant, being born in the likeness of men.*
*And being found in human form he humbled himself*
*and became obedient unto death, even death on a cross.*
– Philippians 2:5–8

How much do you know about gypsies? They're an interesting lot. Custom says they originally may have come out of Egypt, but no one really knows for sure. They had a stint in India as early as 800 A.D. Then they moved throughout Europe and Turkey, and by 1505 had reached England.

Living nomadic, itinerant lives, they did whatever they needed to earn a living. As they traveled from place to place carrying everything they owned in covered wagons and sleeping in tents, they learned to become whatever it took to attend to the needs of each particular community.

In one place they built chair bottoms, made baskets and sharpened knives. In another they mended whatever needed it and caught rats. In still another, they played instruments, sang, danced and put on nightly shows. They have always been a versatile group, to say the least.

In the little town of Panajachel, Guatemala, there is a little restaurant called The Circus Bar that was started by gypsies years ago. Although the present-day owners are not very nomadic, their parents and grandparents were authentic gypsies who did circus-type shows to earn money. There is still a display on a back wall that shows the family with their covered wagon before coming to Guatemala.

The restaurant is very eclectic and has pretty good food to boot. (I'm especially fond of their eggplant dishes ... but that is beside the point.) We do enjoy going there from time to time, especially when we have young people with us. They like to experience the bohemian atmosphere. It is different, that's for sure!

Gypsies have seldom made any bones about their heritage. They are who they are and they do what they have to do — period. It would be interesting to make a comparison between Christians and gypsies. It seems to me that many times we try to blend in with the culture around us. We want to look and act just like everybody else so we won't stand out. Not so with the gypsies. Wherever they go, people quickly recognize them and say, "There go the gypsies!"

I just can't help but wonder what the world would be like if we Christians were more like gypsies in a few regards. What if we were willing to be more mobile and travel to wherever there was a need, and to do whatever it took to reach others for Christ?

The Bible teaches us to go into all the world and make disciples for Christ. Jesus, who left all of heaven's glory and gave up everything to become a servant and offer His life as a sacrifice for us, calls us to have the same mindset. What if we were always on the move and never completely at home in any culture but heaven's? What if we were Christians first, far and beyond any cultural identity of this world? Certainly it would require a tremendous sacrifice on our part, but when did we ever get permission not to make it?

What if we became known wherever we went as a people of great love, service and sacrifice for the good of others? Just imagine people saying:

"Oh good! Finally — here come some Christians!"

"I have some counseling issues that I really need their advice on and several things in my life that desperately need mending, and they can help me."

"I just love it when Christians come to visit. ... All the rats in our lives get chased away, and the nightly gatherings that they put on are just tremendous!"

What a change that would be! Instead, most of us trudge on, trying to protect our "secret" identities, maintaining our daily grinds and trying to not do anything to invade the space of others. A gypsy attitude might help us all!

Awhile back I was seated on a flight beside a woman from the north who was traveling to Panama. We talked for a little while, and she asked me the typical questions "Where are you from?" and "What are you doing here?" and so on. When I told her that I was originally from South Carolina, she fanned her arm across the air as though she were shooing away a bad odor and said, "Why, you can't tell it!"

I guess it was her way of saying, "present company excepted...." I couldn't help but smile. I am actually very proud to be from South Carolina. That is who I am; it's part of my identity. And being a missionary in Guatemala and in

Central America is what I do. I wouldn't want my life to be any other way.

The truth is that in Christ we are now citizens of His kingdom, and we don't fully belong anywhere in this world. And so everywhere we go, it should be our heartfelt desire to be authentic witnesses for our Lord. He has made no mistakes regarding where any of us were born, who we are, or what we do for Him. I believe that it is all according to His plan, and we need not make any excuses for it. I have to believe that God wants to use all our circumstances for His glory. We should be proud of our heritage and our journeys. I want people to know wherever we go who and whose we are. How about you?

Anybody out there got any broken pots that need mending or old knives that need sharpening? Is there brokenness in your life that needs repair? We can help mend lives because we are His, and He can make all things new and straight. Yes, we may live only in covered wagons and we may be only itinerants, but we are here to make a difference! And after we have worked all day, we should spread the word that we are going to have quite an event tonight! Why, there will be singing, dancing, a lot of laughter and a genuine celebration of a people who have been set free to live life in His grace!

Why not come and join us? You too could be a gypsy for Jesus!

# CHAPTER NINE

## Being Useful

# 9.1
## The Power of One

*Then as one man's trespass led to condemnation for all men,*
*so one man's act of righteousness leads to acquittal and life*
*for all men. For as by one man's disobedience many were made*
*sinners, so by one man's obedience many will be made righteous.*
– Romans 5:18–19

*Oh, that there were one among you who would shut the doors,*
*that you might not kindle fire upon my altar in vain!*
– Malachi 1:10a

W E LIVE IN A WORLD where numbers count — the bigger the number, the better, it would seem. Reports, opinion polls and statistical surveys attempt to claim the high ground of public opinion these days by laying claim to a high percentage of numbers that support a particular viewpoint. That viewpoint must be the correct one if enough people feel that way, it is argued. Leaders and organizations often want to get to the bottom line about numbers:

"How are our stats looking?"

"What's the profit margin?"

"What do the numbers say?"

And let's face it. Which impresses you most? The number one — or the number one million?

Call me an oddball, but I happen to be a big fan of the number one. Oh, I wholeheartedly agree with the old song by Three Dog Night that pronounces one "the loneliest number." But it is also a precious number … the most amazing number there is! Especially when we get our perspectives in balance and ask the question, "Compared to what?"

Have you ever considered that there is more difference between the numbers zero and one than there is between one and a million? Consider this: There are more than 7 billion people alive on the planet today. While that number seems pretty amazing (and it is), it pales in comparison to the day when God created the first human being. Just imagine how it was when only the heavens and the Earth and a few animals existed. Then, suddenly, there was man! The beginning of God's favorite creation — a creation so precious that he was instantly the apple of God's eye. (Born at the top of the *Billboard* chart, just like that!)

It was that step between the time when there was nothing and suddenly there was one that made all the difference. One quickly became two, and after two came the 7 billion and more that we have today. Not really that big of a deal, when you think about it. After you reach one it is a relative piece of cake from there. The hard part is getting from zero to one.

And yet one is truly an underrated number. I know many servants of God who feel that they are disappointments because they can count their successes on one hand. And a few successes are just not very impressive nowadays. The world does not give many accolades to accomplishments measured by only small numbers. But God does! When Mordecai Ham preached in a little revival meeting in 1934 and a young lad came forward to accept Christ, I wonder how many there thought their revival meeting was a spectacular success? Just one lad saved. ... But that one turned out to be evangelist Billy Graham! That one decision would later change millions of hearts around the world.

Or consider the plight of a poor Sunday school teacher in a little country church where week after week only one little boy came. She may well have been discouraged, but she pressed on. Week after week, she taught her one little student who seemed bored out of his mind!

One day, however, the light turned on in that little boy's heart, and he heard and understood for the first time about Jesus and His death on the cross to save us. One day that little boy bowed his head in her class and asked Jesus to come into his heart and use him for His glory.

That little boy's name was Bryant Hicks, and he grew up to serve as a Baptist missionary in the Philippines for many years. He later became the Professor of Missions at The Southern Baptist Theological Seminary. Hicks believed in the power of one and had a great influence in so many "ones" who are now in ministries all around the world — including yours truly. He taught me about world missions in seminary and later served as my faculty supervisor in my doctoral studies. Oh, the power and influence of one!

Recently I sat in another little country church in Guatemala where, for different reasons, only the pastor showed up to worship. One man. His wife has all but abandoned her faith. Many of his sons and other church members have turned their backs on their families and on the Lord. Things seem to be falling apart there as many let their apathy and concern for money outweigh their service to God. At times the pastor is all alone in his unwavering faith in Jesus. As a little group of six of us began to sing and worship together there in Pavitzalan, Pastor Genero Lucas had a smile on his face. He joked about being all alone at times in his desire to walk in the ways of Christ.

"Hasta la muerte [Until the death]!" he said.

"It goes further than that," I assured him. "Hasta la vida [To the life everlasting]!"

Yes, one is truly a powerful number. I happen to know that God likes it a lot. Through history, when His servants have stood alone, He has always smiled upon them. We see examples of God working through the prophet Elijah (remember Mount Carmel?) to God's only Son, our Lord Jesus. Unlike ourselves, our Father has always known the true worth of the number one. A faithful "one" beats 7 billion by more than a country mile. By one man, Adam, sin was brought into the world, but by one man, Jesus, our sin debt was settled so that we could be truly free. One is such a big number! Such a glorious number!

Perhaps God is calling you and me to re-learn our numbers. For too long we have been so dazzled with the big numbers that we have forgotten to notice the simple beauty of the little ones. Perhaps the numbers in your life are closer to "one" and you have considered yourself a failure. Think again! "Oh that there were one ... !" the Lord said to Malachi. The trick is to be that "one."

What changes might God bring into this old world with time if one man or one woman will only hold the course and see their work to the end? (Hasta la muerte!) We don't know yet, do we? But I believe that when it is all said and done, we are going to see that one is indeed a beautiful number, a truly extraordinary number ... if it is wholly given over to God's purposes.

My challenge to you is to be the "one." Be the one to make a difference for God — where He has placed you and with the tasks He has given you. Be the one He has made you to be and trust the resulting numbers to Him and to His timing. Oh, the changes He could bring about — all from the power of a faithful "one."

Do you believe this? This is not fuzzy math; this is the gospel. Yes, a million is a good number, too, but the number one is so unique, so life-changing. There is truly nothing like it. May God bless all His "ones" in all the lonely places of the world where they are making a difference. An eternal difference ... .

Press on!

## 9.2
## Footprints on the Ceiling

*"...I will give you the keys to the kingdom of heaven,*
*and whatever you bind on earth shall be bound in heaven,*
*and whatever you loose on earth shall be loosed in heaven."*
– Matthew 16:19

How much influence do you have? Do you know? Many people feel that they have very little influence in the scheme of things, even in their own lives. Perhaps at their job their ideas are ignored or in their families their children can't hear them. As hard as they might try, or as much as they might throw themselves against the wall of their problems, their impact seems minimal. Instead of seeing growth and change as a result of their actions and input, they feel that things just go on and on the same.

They may give up on anyone really being changed by their influence and so resolve to just keep their head down and make it through the day. Day after day, week after week, year after year, they just keep on going and only wishing that they could truly make a difference in this old world. In their hearts, however, they doubt they ever really will.

One such man was named Daniel. Daniel was a decent Christian man who worked very hard to make a difference, but somehow things seldom worked out the way he hoped. Daniel was a farmer in South Carolina with six sons and seven daughters — a big family, even in those days! Despite all his parenting and influence, some of his children chose to live their lives out of a whiskey bottle, leaving hurt and heartbreak as their legacy for all who cared about them. It is a pretty sad story, really.

Work didn't go much better for Daniel. He owned 144 acres of farmland, which he usually planted with cotton. Life was always hard, but he had always managed to eke out a living for his family — that is, until he got hit three consecutive years with uncontrollable cotton weevils. Those three years drove Daniel to desperation. It was then that a man came along and made him an offer on his land. The offer was for a fraction of the land's value, but Daniel was at a low point in his life, and he just couldn't see how he could make it with each new crop failing to bring a profit. So he gave in and sold all his land and went down to apply for a job in the local cotton mill. In his own eyes, he probably considered himself a failure.

Daniel hadn't been able to prevent the heartbreak and failure in his children's lives, and his life's work as a farmer ended in failure as he sold off all his land for a great loss in a desperate time. He lived to a ripe old age and died with dignity, but he never saw his family change, and he never got his land back. I am sure that if you had asked Daniel how his life had turned out, he would have answered with something like, "Not like I thought it would … not at all like I thought it would."

How do I know these things? I know because I am Daniel's grandson. He was my mother's father, and he profoundly impacted my and my brother's lives. He left his mark on us, his young grandsons, and his influence would in many ways help to shape the men that we would become as well as our ministries.

Although he did not pass on land or material goods to us, my grandfather taught us about faith and honor, about keeping your word, and about enjoying life even in difficult circumstances. He also taught us how to fish and how to enjoy the outdoors. He passed along so many keys of understanding that have blessed our lives. Wherever I have traveled in the world, I have remembered his zest for life, his laugh, and his positive character.

My brother, Steve, and I have followed his lead as a role model in dealing with people in many ways. It just goes to show that what we do can influence events that will occur long after we are gone from this world. It might not be like we think it will be, but as Christians our whole lives are contributing to God's plans that will lead on into eternity. We might conclude from our limited perspective that we may have failed, but in God's eyes, those who follow Him always succeed!

Several weeks before my family finished one of our stateside assignments, we took a few days of vacation and went to the beach. It was a wonderful time, as it always is when our family goes there. As we oftentimes do, we had the privilege of staying in the little beach cottage owned by Lily's family. They built it in the early '60s on a wing and a prayer using whatever materials they could scrounge. They got lucky and bought a huge supply of used plywood with which they built the walls and ceilings. Friends and family members put in most of the labor on it. Somehow, it all came together.

One afternoon during our vacation, after eating a wonderful lunch, I retreated to the little daybed that is out on the porch.

With ceiling fans and a light breeze blowing over the porch, it was an ideal place to take a nap. As I lay there, my eyes scanned the plywood ceiling. I chuckled to myself to think that all of the plywood was bought as used lumber from somewhere. There were knots all over it, which you could easily tell because it has been left with its natural finish through the years.

I noticed once again one particular piece of plywood on the ceiling above me. The piece stands out because it has footprints on it! I was about 14 the first time I noticed them, and I remember wondering, *What in the world are footprints doing up there?* Obviously, one of the builders of the cottage had stepped on that piece while it lay on the ground, leaving his shoe print behind. It was a casual thing, certainly not planned. But that shoe print has stayed there on that ceiling now for more than 40 years!

That shoe print started me to thinking. Even though often we are completely unaware of it, what we do down here on the ground has an impact on what goes on above us! We influence others even when we don't have a clue that we are doing so. Our impact on others is much, much greater and longer-lasting than we realize.

Our Lord, in responding to Peter and the other disciples, told them something amazing that they could not understand. Jesus talked to them of His church, which would be established by faith and built upon the hearts of men and women. It would be led by His Holy Spirit, and not even the powers of death could ever prevail against it. Then He went on to tell them that He was placing in their hands the keys to the kingdom of heaven: "… [W]hatever you bind on earth shall be bound in heaven, and whatever you loose on earth shall be loosed in heaven" (Matt. 16:19).

This is an incredible statement! Now, I know that Jesus was talking about the authority and influence of His church and that this instruction goes much deeper than we can really understand right now. But I really believe that in a sense, we, as individual believers, have much more power and influence on others in our world than we realize. I further believe that if we remain faithful to Him, we will have effected changes that we may never even grasp until we stand with our God in heaven and have it all explained to us. It really makes you think, doesn't it?

For now, we must at least look up at the footprints that others have made in our lives and give thanks for all the good that their living the way they lived and their faithfully doing the things they did impacted us. May God grant us the grace and wisdom to consider that what we too do with our lives will make an eternal difference in the lives of others. It is an awesome responsibility, but if our goal in life really is to make a difference for Him, then we have already been granted our desire!

Step on, my brothers and sisters, and let us leave our footprints on the ceilings of others' lives so that they can see that we have walked with Jesus!

## 9.3
## Wooden Legs

*But Moses said to the Lord, "Oh, my Lord, I am not eloquent,*
*either heretofore or since thou has spoken to thy servant;*
*but I am slow of speech and of tongue."*
*Then the Lord said to him, "Who has made man's mouth?*
*Who makes him dumb, or deaf, or seeing, or blind?*
*Is it not I, the Lord? Now therefore go, and I will be with your*
*mouth and teach you what you shall speak."*
– Exodus 4:10–12

SOMEONE ONCE SAID that the true measure of the character of a man could be seen in what it takes to stop him.

Why is it that some people are able to attempt great things for the Lord against seemingly impossible odds, while others with much more facility and giftedness excuse themselves and attempt little in God's service? What factors determine most what we attempt to do in our service of the Lord? In other words, what will it take to stop you and me and to keep us from living out God's plans for us?

It is easy to make excuses and beg off from what we know in our hearts we should be doing. Psychologists call this type of excuse making a "wooden leg." For example, someone might say, "I would really like to help you with that work you're doing, but I can't because I have a wooden leg and can't walk so well." It just a way of saying I'm not going to do what I am supposed to because I can come up with a good excuse that lets me off the hook.

The problem with "wooden leg excuses," of course, is that in spite of our perceived disabilities, we could attempt the task at hand — if we really wanted to. Although our "disabilities" perhaps make it harder to do certain tasks, the thing that really stops us is that we don't want to attempt anything that seems too difficult. Many, however, accomplish incredible things by using what they have and not letting a defeatist attitude stop them from trying. People with literal prosthetic legs work every day, walk normally and even run marathons! There are blind people, deaf people and people with many severe problems who live normal lives and who are successful in many, many fields. As the old saying goes, "Winners are just ordinary people who have extraordinary determination!"

Moses perceived himself as being "slow of speech and tongue." He may have stuttered badly. Yet, in spite of his weakness, God used him to secure the freedom of Israel from the bondage of Egypt. You see, even though Moses tried to excuse himself from being used in God's plan, God would not let him off the hook! The Lord laid claim to Moses' life and told him He would be with him to help him do what he needed to. He also gave him Aaron to help him in the task. In other words, Moses' "wooden leg" (literally his poor speech) was not enough to excuse him from doing what God expected of him.

Please don't get me wrong. Many people suffer from real infirmities that do hinder them. And there are some activities that each of us is just not able to participate in. The problems are real. What is not real, however, is our justification of why we cannot attempt what God asks of us. Sometimes we even take our disability and use it to do just the opposite of what God requires of us.

We once worked with a man who came to Ixchiguan with a leg that was badly infected. This man had diabetes, and his sores were very slow to heal. He showed us his hideous leg (very real indeed!) and asked for a handout. He had done this from town to town and had made a decent living on people's pity.

Instead of giving him money like everybody else, though, we took him into the city to show his leg to a very capable physician who had treated us several times. Dr. Ramirez examined the man and finally told him that he thought he could cure his leg.

The man explained that he had no money and could not afford expensive treatment. Dr. Ramirez told him not to worry. "If you will just do everything that I tell you to do, I will take care of all the rest!" His plan was to place him in the general hospital of Xela (at no cost to the man) and to treat him personally with free but very expensive and very powerful antibiotics that Dr. Ramirez just happened to have. So the patient entered the hospital and was treated for about three days. He started to improve, and the leg was showing results. We were thrilled!

About the third day, however, the patient checked himself out of the hospital and left town. We were flabbergasted! Why would he do that when he was being given free medicine, free hospital care, free treatment and was actually getting better fast! Why would he leave?! He left because he liked using his disability to get a free ride in life. He knew that if he stuck around, his disability would be overcome and he would no

216

longer have any excuse not to do what he was supposed to! Having a "wooden leg" can be pretty useful when we don't want to do the work we should.

In terms of our Christian service, many of us who profess undying faith and obedience to the Lord Jesus find that we have "wooden legs" that excuse us from doing what seems hard to us.

How many people decide not to enter the ministry or missions service because, "I just could never do something like that!" Or, how many people refuse to teach Sunday school, call on the sick, or visit a nursing home because it seems too hard? What about visiting a neighbor and telling her about Jesus? Is there a valid reason why you and I can't even do that? Young people wrestle with deciding on a career, and many resist God's plan to be a nurse or an engineer, for example, because they struggle with math. Do we not believe that God will help us to do anything and everything that He calls us to do ... just as He helped Moses?

What is your "wooden leg"? What is your excuse for not doing the things you know (or at least suspect) in your heart that God wants you to be doing?

Whatever our excuses are, they are not good enough unless God accepts them. Who knows what God could do through ordinary people like you and me if we were to really hand our lives — weaknesses and all — over to His service? We might see people being made free in unexpected places (as in Moses' case) because we let the strength of God work through our weaknesses! Wouldn't it be nice to win "spiritual marathons" for the Lord — wooden legs and all? God may be saying to us, *If you will just do everything I tell you, I will take care of the rest!*

As the great missionary to India, William Carey, once taught us, "Expect great things from God and attempt great things for God!"

... Even with our wooden legs!

## 9.4
## A Time to Run

*Do you not know that in a race all the runners compete,*
*but only one receives the prize? So run that you may obtain it.*
...
*Well, I do not run aimlessly ... .*
– 1 Corinthians 9:24, 26a

Funny, the things that stick in your mind even after many years have passed. For some reason, my mind has held onto a colorful memory that took place when I was about 22 years old.

Lily and I were just getting started as missionary journeymen working in the eastern jungles of Ecuador. We had moved out to the jungle to begin our two years of service there and were trying to get settled in. Lily was working in a little hospital in a town called Coca trying to learn medical Spanish, and I was mostly on the road with my supervisor, James Gilbert, trying to get us some housing built in the little town of Lago Agrio. James and I were on the road a lot in those days, visiting the new missions and working on the site where we hoped we would soon have a place to live.

On this particular day, James had other business, so I stayed alone in Lago Agrio and worked outside clearing weeds and getting the ground prepared for construction. We had agreed that he would come back at the end of the day and pick me up at the

Lago Agrio Church. As I worked along the headwaters of the Amazon basin, I quickly became hot, tired and stressed out. The sun really took it out of me.

By the end of the day, I was flat worn out. I was filthy, dehydrated and I could barely walk. The one thing on my mind was finding James and getting out of there. I had had enough for one day. It was a surprise to me, then, that when I looked at my watch, it was already past the time for James to pick me up. I finished up my work and hurried to the spot where we had agreed to meet.

While I was still a good way off, I saw James' brown pickup parked in front of the church. He was there waiting for me. As I got a little closer, however, I saw to my dismay that he had apparently given up waiting and was pulling away! I started to run, wave my arms and yell, but he couldn't see me. James was my only chance to get back to civilization; otherwise I would have to stay the night alone in Lago Agrio. I saw the pickup go around the corner from the church, and I ran faster. I knew that my only hope was to cut through the next street and head off the truck before James got away.

Even though I was exhausted, I knew that I had to run and run hard. So I did. I finally caught up to the rear of the vehicle, where I continued to yell for him to stop. He still couldn't see or hear me. I then did the only thing I could think of. I ran as close to the rear of the truck as I could and threw myself into the back of it. That was when James finally heard me and stopped the truck. My running had paid off.

Such an odd little memory. ... And yet it does remind me of something. We spend most of our lives running from one thing to the next. We get tired and we complain, yet we just keep on going. The problem is that often our running doesn't get us anywhere. So many people run and don't know what they are running for. It's just the way they live.

Paul talked about a different way of living. He described his own goal of running so that he might obtain the "imperishable wreath." In other words, he wanted his life to count for something that was worth living for — and worth dying for. He didn't run for lack of good planning. Neither did he run just because he liked to or because anyone else made him. He had his sights set on the kingdom of God, and he ran with all his might until it was time for him to go home.

In the times when we get weary, we sometimes forget what we are supposed to be running for. From time to time we need to refocus on the goal and keep on running hard. Life is a race. There is a beginning, an end, and only a limited time to run. As for me, I don't know how to accomplish anything without running. There are too many things that need to be done. It is my hope, however, to not "run aimlessly." I, like Paul, want my running to always be for a reason: to receive the prize for which God put me upon this Earth. I want my life to count for great things. I am not willing to just get through the day. I want to get the job done and then go home.

Run. But run for a reason. Don't run anywhere that takes you away from the path that God has for you. Don't give up. Take heart, in spite of the heat or the weariness. After all, we as Christians are running the greatest race on Earth, and we are running it for a purpose. Make each day count.

The finish line awaits us!

## 9.5
## Things My Dog Taught Me
🍃

*But he who is joined with all the living has hope,*
*for a living dog is better than a dead lion.*
— Ecclesiastes 9:4

*"By [Silas], a faithful brother as I regard him ...."*
— 1 Peter 5:12a

THE GROUND HAS GOTTEN QUITE HARD, now that the rains have stopped. I know this because I have just finished digging a grave behind the shed in my backyard.

*I wish it were still raining,* I think as I wipe the sweat from my brow and lean back on my shovel to rest for a moment. It certainly feels as though it should be raining now. Who are we, though, to decide the timing of such things? Things happen when they happen ... that's all there is to it. Still, the hard ground of our emotions must make way for death, whether we are ready for it or not.

*Silas*, I say to myself, for there is no one else around to hear me. *You were a good dog!*

After lowering him into his grave, I cover him with a handsome little white towel with pink, purple and green flowers on it that I like to think he would have liked. After this, I fill in the hole with dirt and smooth it out.

Without warning I am joined by our two new puppies, Marley and Rasta. The pups watch for a minute and then trudge away as if they somehow understand that Silas is no more.

For 13 years he blessed our lives. Being a purebred boxer, he was a beautiful dog. He originally belonged to some friends of ours in Guatemala City, and we enjoyed playing with Silas when he was a small puppy. Then, when his owners moved into a house with a smaller backyard, they offered him to us. We were living in the mountain village of Ixchiguan full-time then and had plenty of room for him to run and play. So he became our dog and lived with us and guarded our house for these many years.

Recently, though, when we returned from the States, we found Silas sickly, thin and close to death. We brought him down the mountain to live the remainder of his days in Xela with us. We cared for him as best we could, taking him to the vet, giving him raw eggs and tasty morsels to put some meat back on his poor bones, and showering him with attention. I am glad that he lived his final months happily in the community of our motley crew of dogs, family and visitors.

Someone once said that you can't teach an old dog new tricks. That might be so, but I have come to believe that an old dog can certainly teach us humans a thing or two. There are so many things that Silas taught our family … about honor and duty, about being responsible, and about enjoying life.

Here are seven of the lessons Silas taught us:

1. Be a leader!
   Silas never was one to sit back and let someone else tell him what to do. He decided for himself what needed to be done, and he did it … at times whether we liked it or not.

Other dogs that came near him learned very quickly that Silas was no pushover. The cats that came around did not stay long. Mules that wandered into our yard were led around by him all over the grounds. He was proactive instead of reactive to the events around him. He was the kind of dog that made things happen wherever he went!

2. Always be faithful and do your duty!
Silas always knew whose dog he was. He was faithful to stay with us, guard our home and protect us. He accepted his role, and it fit him very well. I only wish that I could follow his example in service and that I were as faithful to the Lord as Silas was to me.

3. Welcome the good and separate yourself from the bad!
Silas always had an uncanny ability for knowing who to welcome into our yard and whom not to allow. During the day, he permitted little children and needy women to walk right by him through our gate. Certain characters, though, would be counted as foes, and he would stand and bark and bark at them until we came to decide whether to let them in or not. He would also become very fierce after dark, and he screened everything that passed by. He didn't want any bad thing getting through on his watch, so he proudly took his position on the front line to keep any evildoers at bay. I wish I had his ability to discern the good from the bad and to keep evil at bay.

4. Chase the light!
Almost anyone who knew Silas knew that he loved the light. A favorite game of his was to follow a beam of light anywhere it went. We would shine flashlights or let the reflection of our watches catch Silas' eye just for the pleasure of seeing him go wild! He would wag his tail

(or rather the piece of it he had left) and follow the light straight up a brick wall with glee. Silas taught us to love the light and to follow it anywhere it leads.

5. Eat waffles every chance you get!
   I have never known anyone (person, dog or other) to enjoy eating waffles as much as Silas. Anytime Lily made them, Silas would go crazy! If he was outside, he would come over and "stand up" on our washing machine so he could stare straight into our kitchen window. He would focus on those lovely waffles being cooked and bark until he was offered some. He could never get enough for truly waffles were a major love of his life. I wish that I had the boldness to go after the wonderful things of life with the gusto Silas went after waffles.

6. Love deeply!
   Silas was such an affectionate dog! He lived for getting petted and for being near people because he genuinely enjoyed being with them. Mission teams always adored him because he would get right up in their laps and beg for their attention with those big old beaming eyes that he had and with those two little bottom teeth that always seemed to be visible when he wanted attention. He just enjoyed being near those whom he loved and would stay near them as long as he could. I wish that I could love people and appreciate them for who they really are as Silas did. I wish that I could keep my focus on people instead of on things or activities of my life and that I could love deeply as Jesus taught us to.

7. Finish life with grace and dignity!
   Throughout Silas' life, he embodied dignity. As a young pup, he was wild and full of energy. As a grown

dog, he held his head high and pranced through the yard with flare. Even in his old age, Silas had a quiet dignity about him. When we brought in Marley and Rasta to live with us, they would bounce on top of him and nip at him. He took all this in stride and even let them lie on top of him as he slept. Somehow, he knew that he had to share with them and to teach them how to get along with others. Even in his time of death, I'll never forget how he walked out of our kitchen with his head up. He went around to the far corner of the house and died there as though he did not want to upset our family by dying in front of us. Silas makes me want to finish the days of my life with grace and dignity and while being a blessing to those around me. I want to be as the apostle Paul described in 1 Corinthians 16:13–14: "Be watchful, stand firm in your faith, be courageous, be strong. Let all that you do be done in love."

Yes, there are so many lessons that Silas has taught me. He was only a dog, and yet he served as a reminder to me of the importance of staying focused on the most important things in life. It may sound silly, but his life challenged me to be a better person. Who would have thought it?

Have your pets taught you anything important lately?

# CHAPTER TEN

## Smiling Again

# 10.1

## Laughing at Ourselves:
## What To Do When Our Good Ideas Don't Work Out

*But Moses said to the Lord, "Oh, my Lord,*
*I am not eloquent, either heretofore or since*
*thou hast spoken to thy servant;*
*but I am slow of speech and of tongue."*
– Exodus 4:10

*Many are the plans in the mind of a man,*
*but it is the purpose of the Lord that will be established.*
– Proverbs 19:21

*A word fitly spoken is like apples of gold*
*in a setting of silver.*
– Proverbs 25:11

WE ALL DESIRE TO SPEAK a good word from the Lord and to pass it on to those whom God has placed within our hearing. Yet as much as we may wish to tell the story, sing the song, teach the lesson or preach the sermon in the best way possible, most of us at one time or another have totally blown it! Rather than being eloquent and provoking deep thought in the more profound things of God, we have used the wrong word, hit the wrong note, or fumbled through an illustration and left people surprised, embarrassed or guffawing in their seats.

228

Have you ever had that experience? If you're going to be in front of the public very long, you had better be prepared to be laughed at. It's going to happen.

Moses realized that he couldn't always get the right words out. When God called him to be His spokesman to the leaders of Egypt in securing the freedom of the Hebrews, Moses could see it coming. He was going to mess up. He just knew it. And he wisely prepared for that eventuality by confessing his fallibility to the Lord ahead of time.

Missionary life is full of language mistakes. When I preached my first sermon in Spanish at a little jungle village called Chiritza back in 1980, I caused quite a stir. It was supposed to be a sermon focused on the cross and the events surrounding Easter. However, apparently my Spanish was so bad that several people got completely lost and had no idea whatsoever what I was trying to get across. Yet one old man named Deker (who was completely blind) appeared to be right with me and he became very concerned and nodded his head as I preached. I thought that he was really moved by my sermon and by the events of Holy Week. He was especially attentive while I talked about Pontius Pilate and about his role in handing Jesus over to the crowds to be crucified. At least one person was really paying attention to my sermon, I consoled myself. So I preached my heart out to Brother Deker.

After my message was over, Deker made his way over to me looking like a blind Charlton Heston in some Moses movie. He was about 80 years old and had a long, flowing, white beard. Because of his blindness, he held his head tilted slightly upward and carried the general appearance that he just might be one of the Old Testament prophets come back to life. Holding his cane in one hand and grasping mine with his other, he congratulated me on a "fine sermon!"

"Tell me, though," he pleaded with a deeply concerned expression on his face, "did that pilot who crashed out here in the jungle live or die?"

Another time, a close friend of mine named Rod had cooked up a brilliant children's sermon. It was aimed at helping young children become aware of the work of the Holy Spirit. He talked about how many marvelous things in life are not easily visible and understood at first glance. The Holy Spirit can't be seen with human eyes or touched with human hands, and yet He is very real and very present in the life of the believer — just like music. Music is in the air all around us in the AM and FM waves, but we don't always hear it, do we?

"Do you believe, boys and girls, that there is music floating through the air right now but that you are not hearing it because you are not tuned in?" Rod asked them.

He had a radio all cued up on a certain channel, and when the right time came he was going to just twist the button and turn it on, letting them hear the beautiful music that he had just "tuned in." To this day, I do not know what happened, but when he got to the crucial part of his message and bent over and twisted the knob on his radio, nothing happened. Zip. Zilch. Nada!

There was total silence while he turned it off and on several times and as he checked all the wires and plugs. At first he was embarrassed, and then he got more and more frustrated that the thing wouldn't work! You could tell from his eyes that he was ready to chuck the radio out the window! The more upset he got, the funnier the whole thing was. By the end, there was not a dry eye in the place! We were howling with laughter!

Speaking of children's sermons gone wrong .... This time it was a youth minister who wanted to teach on the Holy Spirit in his children's sermon. He apparently wanted to get across the message that one of the roles of the Holy Spirit is to draw people closer to Jesus. So he designed this odd-looking box to represent the Holy Spirit and put it at the front of the church. He then gave each child a little slip of paper. What they didn't know was that he had hooked up a vacuum cleaner behind the box and had it set to suck up each little slip of paper when each kid held it near enough to a little slot in the box. He talked to the group and assured them that the Holy Spirit was real and that He would do really neat things if we would draw near enough to Him. At that, he asked the first child to hold his slip of paper directly in front of the slot in the big box, and then he turned on the vacuum cleaner.

*Vvvrrrrooooooommm!!* The box erupted in a deafening roar. The poor little kid was scared to death! He let out a yelp, dropped his piece of paper, and ran down the aisle of the church toward his mama.

The other kids were frightened, too, and there was no way they were going to get their arms anywhere near that thing in the box — it might eat off their arms!

Every adult in the place howled with laughter! The embarrassed youth minister quickly wrapped up his message, but we had a great time! Another fantastic memory was made.

What do we do when we mess up and become the laughingstock of a group of people? Our first temptation is to become embarrassed. Then we might get frustrated or even angry — at ourselves, at a gadget's faulty plug, or an overly noisy old vacuum cleaner!

I have certainly experienced those emotions when my messages have not worked out the way I wanted them to. However, something comes to my mind when I remember all my mess-ups. As embarrassing as they might be for the leader, they are often the most memorable lessons that we ever get! I will never forget the above situations or the actual intended messages they were designed to convey! I suspect that at least one of the stories above will stay with you for a long while as well. Just think about it. The ordinary that always works as expected is not very memorable. But the unexpected times, the hilarious times ... these will be etched in our brains all our days.

Maybe we should be glad when our best efforts mess up from time to time. Maybe God can use even those times to get His point across. I know; we don't want to mess up. It hurts our pride. But if we can get to the point of not taking ourselves so seriously, we might just find those times even funnier than those around us. After all, "Many are the plans in the mind of a man, but it is the purpose of the Lord that will be established" (Prov. 19:21). And that's what really matters.

So the next time you mess up and really embarrass yourself in front of others, just remember that you might just be providing them with a memorable moment that will teach them (or even yourself!) your lesson better than you could have ever imagined! Who knows how God may use even our worst foul-ups?

Don't worry so much about how you perform. Just be faithful and carry on. He's got you covered!

## 10.2
### It's a Strange World After All ...

*When they came to Capernaum, the collectors*
*of the half-shekel tax went up to Peter and said, "Does not your*
*teacher pay the tax?"*
*He said, "Yes."*
...
*Jesus said to him ... "[G]o to the sea and cast a hook, and take*
*the first fish that comes up, and when you open its mouth you will*
*find a shekel; take that and give it to them for me and for yourself."*
– Matthew 17:24, 25a, 26a, 27b

---

*And behold, men were bringing on a bed a man who was paralyzed*
*... but finding no way to bring him in, because of the crowd,*
*they went up on the roof and let him down with his bed*
*through the tiles into the midst before Jesus.*
– Luke 5:18a, 19

WE MAY HAVE A DOUBT or two about the claim of a Disney theme park ride that this is a "small world after all," but I, for one, have no doubt that it's certainly a strange one! Things out of the ordinary happen all the time — and I'm so glad that they do! I'm happy that God has a sense of humor and that He doesn't choose to do things the same old way every time. Every day is a new day, fresh with any number of possibilities. It makes one want to get out of bed in the morning just to see what is going to happen next, doesn't it?

Take the life and times of my father-in-law, Bill Pascoe, for example. He has had more strange happenings in his life than almost anyone else I know. Several years ago, he was cutting grass in front of his house when he felt a sharp sting on his earlobe. Because he was beneath a small tree with its limbs hanging down around his head, his first thought was that a snake lounging on one of the limbs may have bitten him.

Thinking to get away from the snake, he jerked his head away from the tree. It hurt worse! He reached up to feel his earlobe and discovered that completely piercing his ear was a fishhook — still attached to a fishing line and sinker. When he went to his doctor to get it removed, the doctor casually asked where Bill had been fishing when it happened. "Fishing!" he responded, "I was cutting the grass!"

Another time, Bill had had some major lung surgery and was recovering at home. He owned a couple of dogs, and from time to time one of the local grocery stores would give him huge bones for them. Even though Bill knew he wasn't supposed to be exerting himself following his surgery, he decided to make his dogs happy and chop up some of the bones.

He got his axe and placed a big bone on the ground in his backyard. He hadn't noticed that while he had been in the hospital, his wife Lucy had had a new clothesline installed, and it was right over where he was attempting to cut the bones. He drew back the axe, only to have it catch on the clothesline overhead. As he applied pressure to bring it down on the bones, it pulled the steel clothesline down a ways with it, causing the axe to slip from its path and to nick him in the head.

Then the steel clothesline popped back to its place — taking the axe with it. The axe flew out of Bill's hands and into the air,

234

twirling and catching him on the head as it ascended. The blow dropped him to his knees. From there, he tilted his head to look up and see where the axe had gone. It was spinning downward straight toward his head. He could only stare in amazement as it came down, dull side first (thank the Lord!), and whacked him on the head yet again.

With several head wounds to go with his recent lung surgery, he had to confess what he had done to his wife and go for some stitches. Can't you imagine the strange looks of the nurse and the doctor who wrote up the report on that one?

During one of our vacations during the month of August, we stayed in a very nice little inn where they stocked the refrigerator with complimentary goodies and free drinks. Lily's parents stayed in the room directly under us. As we were checking out of the inn, Lily's dad decided to take a complimentary bottle of Italian sparkling water home with him. After getting back home, he placed the big bottle in a corner beside the refrigerator.

A day or two later, Lily's mom was talking on the phone in the kitchen when she heard what sounded like a small explosion nearby. She looked around and saw glass littering the floor and countertops. As she and Bill searched for the cause of the explosion, they found that the innocuous bottle of water, sitting alone, had burst. How often do you have to worry about a bottle of water exploding in your kitchen? As Bill said to us afterward, "You can't protect yourself against everything. You never know when a bottle of water might explode!"

It must run in the family. Not long ago Lily was working in our kitchen. As she was cooking, somehow a box of salt in the cabinet became unsettled and fell onto the counter right beside her where a fork rested. When the salt landed, it caught the tines of the fork and sent it sailing through the air, where it snagged Lily's bottom lip, penetrating it completely. She wasn't really hurt badly, but she was shaken up. Try dropping a box of salt out of your cabinet onto a fork below and see how many times you have to do it before you can send it flying through your lower lip.

Uh-huh ... strange things do happen in our family.

Not too long ago, a team member from Spartanburg, South Carolina stayed in the little apartment (what we call "the Chalet") below our house in Ixchiguan. On the last day, he dressed, packed and headed down the mountain with the rest of the team. Along the way, he complained to one of the doctors on the team that he was having some "toe spasms" that made his toes twitch.

The doctor told him it probably wasn't anything to worry about. So beyond attacking his itchy toes with fits of vigorous scratching from time to time, he basically just lived with the itchy twitching until the team arrived in Xela.

Once he arrived, he decided to take a bounce on the trampoline in our backyard. He removed his shoes and, lo and behold, the body of a fairly large green lizard fell out! Apparently it had crawled into his shoe before he dressed that morning, and it had been trapped, twitching, for hours before it finally succumbed, poor thing. We still don't know if the scratching or foot odor killed it. Yep, it's a strange world after all.

Another offbeat thing happened during a medical clinic in Estrella Blanca. Hundreds of people had come from several neighboring villages to be seen by the doctors. One young man arrived with his grandmother tied onto his back. She was sitting

236

in a little wooden chair, and the chair was tied onto her grandson's back. He had walked more than 6 miles uphill to get her to the clinic, and although it was chilly, he was covered with sweat. His grandmother had suffered a stroke some time back and he, along with his grandfather, wanted to see if there was any hope for her. In addition to seeking medical help, the young man had heard about Jesus and wanted to find out more. Jesus and our group of Christian doctors represented his last hope for his grandmother.

The doctors regretted that there was not much that they could do for her body. Her blood pressure was about 200 over 120. She was in bad shape, and it was just a matter of time. Lily and the team began to witness to the grandmother, grandfather and grandson. Jeronimo and Lucio talked to them in Mam to make sure they understood the offer of salvation through Jesus Christ. After careful thought, all three prayed to receive Christ in that little mountain village! Jesus came into their hearts right then and there.

How many of us could or would carry someone (even our own grandmother) on our backs for 6 miles in order to hear about Jesus? Such a strange thing to do! It reminds me of the four friends who carried their sick friend to see Jesus. When they realized they couldn't get to Him because of the crowds, they made a hole in the roof of the house and lowered him in front of Jesus. Because of their strange efforts, salvation came to their paralyzed friend that day. Just like it came to the house of a crippled grandmother.

Yes, it is a strange world after all. ... Strange things happen every day to those who believe. And we are so glad that they do! I wouldn't want it any other way. Would you?

## 10.3
### How to Cope with Change

*For their rock is not as our Rock....*
— Deuteronomy 32:31a

*But I trust in thee, O Lord, I say, "Thou art my God."*
*My times are in thy hand....*
— Psalms 31:14–15a

M̲Y BROTHER, STEVE, realized just the other day that it was time for a change. He was at the cleaners picking up a suit, and the lady behind the counter looked at him a little strangely and confessed that "there had been a little problem."

"You might notice that your suit fits a little more snugly now than it used to," she told him.

"Oh?" he asked. "Why is that?"

"Well ... we had to do a little sewing down the back."

Steve turned the suit over to look at the back and saw a tremendous tear from the top to the bottom that had been sewn together. It looked terrible!

"What in the world happened to my suit coat?" he asked.

"Well, it was all a big mistake," she replied confidentially. "Somehow your suit got sent to the mortuary instead of another one that we were supposed to send. I called them as soon as I realized that we had made the mistake — but they told me that it was already too late!"

238

"You can't have the suit back now!" the man at the mortuary had told her. "The back of the suit has already been slit, and it is now being used!"

"I don't care!" she said sternly. "I've got to have Mr. Stone's suit back. You'll just have to change it!"

So the morticians had to take Steve's suit off the recently deceased gentleman in his coffin and return it to the dry cleaners where it would be re-sewn, re-cleaned and re-hung on the rack, packaged up in a pristine little plastic bag for my brother to come and pick it up.

Yep. Steve knew right then that it was time to make a change and get a new suit — as well as a new dry cleaner!

Sometimes changes sneak up on us, and we have to cope with them whether we want to or not. Time is perhaps the biggest initiator of change in our lives. I remember several years ago when I turned 40 and went for an eye exam. The optometrist examined me and asked if my sight was getting significantly blurrier.

"No," I told him. "Not that I've noticed."

"Well, it will be soon," he said. "Don't be surprised if your vision starts going downhill soon now that you've turned forty."

Boy, he wasn't kidding! Not long after that visit, my vision started falling apart.

A few days ago I went to get my license renewed. Although I had never had to wear my glasses to pass the eye test before, I was concerned that this time might be different. Sure enough, when I looked into the little machine, I couldn't read a single line!

*This is bad!* I thought, and reached into my pocket and pulled out my old glasses that I had gotten for distance vision (and which I hardly ever used). Explaining to the clerk that I did sometimes need my glasses now, I put them on and looked into the machine — only to find that I still couldn't read all the letters.

*This is not just bad...this is really bad!* I thought. I squinted and squirmed and after a bit was able to make out all of the letters on the first line — except one. I saw the letter, and it looked exactly like an "O" to me. I told the lady as much, and she told me that I was wrong.

"It sure looks like an 'O,'" I told her.

"Yes, but it is not an 'O,'" she told me with a grade-school teacher smile.

So I started getting creative. "Is it a 'P?'"

"No."

"Is it an 'R?'"

"No."

"Are you sure it's not an 'O?'"

"No, it is not an 'O.'"

At that point my situation was getting pitiful. The lady had written what the letter was on a piece of paper and shown it to Lily, who then said, "Gary, why don't you repeat your A-B-C's?", giving the last letter a peculiar emphasis.

"Is it a 'D?'" I asked as though I were a contestant on a game show hoping to soon buy a vowel.

"No."

The situation was getting pretty pathetic when Lily again said to me, "Gary, just remember your A-B-*Sees*!!"

"Is it a 'Q?'"

"No."

After a couple more wrong guesses, I knew that she was about to reach behind the counter and hit the gong on me.

240

"Is it a 'C'"? I asked.

Following my many pitiful attempts, the poor lady had so zoned out that she didn't even hear me.

"He said 'C!'" Lily cried. "He said it was a 'C!'"

Had I not had the kindest clerk on the planet, I would have walked out of there without a license. It was definitely time to get my glasses changed! (For those on recent mission teams with me, this drivers license experience should do much to explain a few of my "hello!" moments.)

When your vision begins to go, you get a little antsy, asking yourself what will go next.

I should have never asked.

Just the other day I ran into an old friend from high school whom I had not seen in quite a while who has been working as a dentist for many years. We walked out of a church service together and began to talk about how the years had gone by.

"So, you're still a missionary?" he asked with a smile.

"Yep, I am," I replied. "I wouldn't want to be anything else! You know, life is short and we don't have forever to accomplish what God put us on this Earth to do. We really have to seek God's will for us and, once we find it, do it with all our heart!"

It was then that I heard him say, "I still feel called to ministry."

"Oh, really!" I said excitedly. "I never knew that! That's wonderful! You know, there are so many needs in this world. The harvest is truly plentiful and the laborers are so few. So many churches are looking for pastors, both full-time and part-time. There are so many ways that you could serve. You know, there's no time to waste! If you really feel that way, you had better move on it as soon as you can!"

It was then that I finally noticed that his eyes had gotten quite a bit larger. "Dentistry," he said.

"What?" I asked.

"I said that I still feel called to *dentistry!*"

"Oh ..."

The eyes, the ears ... what next? All I know is that change is inevitable in our lives for as long as we go on living. The best way to stop changing is to die! But most of us prefer option A: learning to somehow cope with change for a while longer.

What's the best way to cope with change? I'm not sure I know. But I can tell you what I think. Three things seem to help me. The first is faith in Christ. Because of our faith, we must put what we believe into practice as we face the changes in our lives. As the Serenity Prayer goes, "God grant me the serenity to accept the things I cannot change, courage to change the things I can, and wisdom to know the difference." There is a lot of truth in that prayer!

A second tool for us to use in coping with change is an ongoing sense of humility. Change happens to everybody else, so why shouldn't it happen to us? Why should our lives stay the same? Change is just part of reality, and we must accept and cope with it like everyone else. As Christians, in fact, we have the advantage of better coping mechanisms. We can do it! God will help us find a way. Let's not take ourselves or our situations too seriously. The changes are not always bad; sometimes they lead to new opportunities and new beginnings! Staying humble can keep us in a frame of mind where we can accept and even celebrate many of the changes that take place in our lives.

A third tool to get us through the changes that we must face is a good sense of humor. Some people act as if their sense of humor is broken! Now, that is really bad! If we get to where we can't look at ourselves and laugh a little, then we are really in bad shape. So come on! Let's look for the humor in some of our situations. Laughter never really hurt anyone. It is a God-given, natural way to relieve stress and cope with change. Those who laugh more usually tend to have lower stress levels and lower blood pressure, and they live longer as well as enjoy their lives more!

So keep your faith intact when you go through life's changes. Stay humble. And look for the humor in the changing stories of our lives. Life is not always a struggle to be endured. Sometimes it really is a marvelous adventure to be enjoyed! Let's do so!

By the way, my brother still has a good suit for sale that's only been worn by him and one other guy. I can give you his phone number if you're interested. He would also like to ask if anyone knows of another good dry cleaners.

Keep smiling!

## 10.4
## Lights in the Darkness

*Arise, shine; for your light has come, and the glory of the Lord*
*has risen upon you. For behold, darkness shall cover the earth,*
*and thick darkness the peoples; but the Lord will arise upon you,*
*and his glory will be seen upon you. And nations shall come*
*to your light, and kings to the brightness of your rising.*
*– Isaiah 60:1–3*

During the mid-'70s, Lily and I served as summer missionaries on Hunting Island, South Carolina for three summers. We lived in the middle of the campground on a slight hill in a little Zipper camper that measured about 6 by18 feet. We were on our honeymoon when we first went to work there in June 1975, and we did not mind the small living space.

All of the other campsites were connected on one electric line, but because we were set up beside a pumphouse where they let us keep a little freezer (for the multitudes of fish we caught — yeah, right), we were on a different electrical connection. No one knew this or cared to know it until one special evening.

About once or twice each summer along the coast of South Carolina, terrible rainstorms hit. One week it started raining, and it just did not want to quit. It rained and rained and flooded the campsites. The wind blew hard and tore down tree limbs, causing the electric lines to go down. One night the park lost its main electrical connection, and the campsites were cast in total darkness — except for our little camper.

Because of our special pumphouse connection, our camper was just glowing away through the darkness. We were minding our own business when we became aware that a large crowd had gathered outside. They were staring at our lights in amazement.

We overheard someone ask, "How come they have lights when nobody else does?"

Someone answered them in a near whisper, "Don't you know? They're the Christian chaplains here — no wonder they have lights. You'd better be nice to them or lightning might strike you!"

We have chuckled at that memory through the years. But you know, we have something of the same situation in our everyday lives, don't we? You and I are connected to a different source of power from the rest of the world. All around us there are storms and darkness, but in our hearts we have a light that will not go out. If we stay plugged in, the light will shine through us, and, given enough time, the world will take notice and be drawn to that light.

The difficult part, of course, is letting His light shine brightly through us. Sometimes we let it grow dim because we walk far away from His will. At other times, we almost seem ashamed that we have light when no one else does. Some among us even forget what the light is for and think it is for our benefit alone.

We need to remember the Lord's command: "Arise, shine; for your light has come, and the glory of the Lord has risen upon you." It is a really dark world out there, and unless the peoples of our world see the light in us, how will they be drawn to Him and be saved?

Shine on, my brothers and sisters. Shine on!

## 10.5
## An End to Evangelism!

*"... This is the covenant that I will make with the house of Israel after those days, says the Lord: I will put my laws into their minds, and I will write them on their hearts, and I will be their God, and they shall be my people. And they shall not teach every one his fellow or every one his brother, saying 'Know the Lord,' for all shall know me, from the least of them to the greatest...."*
– Hebrews 8:10–11

How do you feel when you hear the word "evangelism"? Some of us preacher- and missionary-types talk about it an awful lot. Not everyone has as good a reaction to the word as the rest of us, though. Evangelize your neighbor! Evangelize the people in China! Evangelize Iraq! Evangelize the Tajumulco Mam! Evangelize me, evangelize you!

Some churches seem to believe that evangelism is a rotten task but that somebody has to do it. Usually that "somebody" is a paid minister or missionary. By paying someone, it is believed, the church member can be relieved of personal responsibility to tell the whole world about Jesus.

I and a fellow missionary named Keith Stamps once had some responsibilities at a church event in Tejutla, Guatemala. It was a two-day affair, and neither Keith nor I could be there for the whole event. So we decided to split it up. Keith would take the first day, and I would take the second. When I arrived on the second day, though, someone told me that Brother Stamps was still there. I was puzzled because I knew that he had to return home the previous evening.

"He's still here?" I asked. "Where is he?"

"Oh, he is out evangelizing!" the brother told me. "He's been out evangelizing since yesterday, and he just hasn't come back yet!"

Obviously the brother I was speaking with was not out evangelizing. He was right there with everybody else. But Brother Keith was a spiritual hero to him because he was out doing the work of evangelism so that he did not have to do it! Seen in this light, evangelism must truly be an odious task … one that only salaried churchmen or "Super Christians" would attempt!

Many express dislike for the term "evangelism" because it carries other meanings for them. Some who hear the word think "proselytizing," or stealing people away from their church to yours. Others hear "Bible banging" or think of pushy "headhunters" who are looking for another notch on their belts to report back to those who sent them out. Sometimes it makes people think of immature Christians with a shallow, canned presentation who go out to "talk at" their listeners in order to win them over to their point of view instead of "talking with" them. Some people look at those who go out to evangelize as though they were a salesperson trying to sell them a used car from Honest Ed's Car Emporium.

I remember while serving in Australia that a traveling salesman came to call on us at our home in Katherine. As he was climbing the steps to the front door, he saw me at the top of the stairs and called out, "Don't worry, I'm not a churchie!" (a term for Christians that carries all the bad baggage that you can imagine).

"That's okay," I told him with a smile. "I am."

You should have seen the horrified look on his face! After we had visited for a little while, he left (I hope) with at least a little better concept of what a Christian is. So many people just don't get it when it comes to what Christianity is all about! And often those of us who are charged with making Christ known to the world don't do a very good job of representing Him.

Often the Christian community uses other words connected with evangelism that to the unconverted world sound pretty scary, such as: "cultivate," "target," or to "infect" with the gospel. Are non-believers plants that we would "cultivate" them? Are they military objectives to be targeted? Is the gospel a disease that we would infect people with it? I think not. We talk about "winning" people. Do we mean that Jesus wins them, or are we the ones who win by having them agree with us? Is the truth not that when one receives Jesus into his/her heart that we all become winners — the new believer because he has just been forgiven and has received eternal life with the Lord, and us because we have a new brother or sister we will enjoy knowing forever?

When I was a little boy, a man came by our house with a truck of watermelons to sell. It was fascinating to see the mountain of watermelons piled up in his truck along with all the other produce. He saw me staring at him as my dad bought a watermelon, and the man jokingly said he was going to put me in one of his bags and carry me away with him in his truck. I was terrified and ran away screaming! The idea of someone capturing me, putting me into their bag and carrying me away with them was about the worst thing I could think of. I still don't like that idea.

I have wondered from time to time if perhaps some of the people with whom we try to share about the Lord have the same sensation ... that we are engaging them with our smiles while at the same time holding a sack behind our backs and whispering under our breaths, "Heeere, sinner, sinner, sinner ... ."

Now don't get me wrong! You would be hard-pressed to find anyone who is more committed to evangelism than I am! The Great Commission of our Lord demands that we go out and make disciples of all peoples, leading them from darkness into the light of Jesus Christ, and I have spent most of my life trying to do just that. I wonder, though, if we wouldn't be more effective if we were more real and less "churchy"? Wouldn't our evangelism efforts be more effective if they were from our hearts and genuinely motivated by our passion to share the best thing in our lives with people we sincerely care about?

After all, the real meaning behind the word "evangelize" is to spread the gospel, to tell the good news! Our goal is to help people put their faith in Jesus so that their sins will be forgiven, so that they may have new life with excitement, joy and purpose in His plan, and that they might have a personal, ongoing relationship with Jesus!

There shouldn't be a "bag" behind our backs. There shouldn't be any fine print below the dotted line. What we have to share is truly, without doubt, the most wonderful thing in all of life! We don't need to experiment with different "packaging" as we share the gospel; the product is rock-solid, and it's a commodity no one in the world can live without!

Hebrews 8 tells us of a time when there won't be any need to tell the good news to anyone. They will already know it for they will already know Him! However, that time has not yet come! Meanwhile, tell everyone you know — tell everyone you don't know — that God loves sinners and that Jesus wants to pay the debt they cannot pay and to give them the life they have always dreamed of: eternal life lived out under God's plan! Take heart. The product that you and I are called to distribute is the best in the world and one that everyone must have!

So forget about "evangelizing" and today just go out and tell everybody you can the good news of Jesus! If we will just do that, those who hear the gospel will be glad that we did!

CHAPTER ELEVEN

Searching for Understanding

## 11.1

## A Return to Learning Things
## We Never Knew We Never Knew

*I praise thee, for thou art fearful and wonderful.*
*Wonderful are thy works!*
– Psalm 139:14a

*At that time the disciples came to Jesus, saying,*
*"Who is the greatest in the kingdom of heaven?"*
*And calling to him a child, he put him in the midst of them, and said,*
*"Truly, I say to you, unless you turn and become like children,*
*you will never enter the kingdom of heaven."*
– Matthew 18:1–3

Made any new goals for self-improvement lately? In addition to losing weight, working smarter, being bolder, getting more exercise, and the rest of the usual list, I want to encourage you to add one more goal. Would you consider joining me in striving to discover more of the greatness of God's working in our world?

Children are experts in this area. They spend their early years noticing everything around them, and their lips constantly form questions such as: "What is that?" "How come birds fly?" "What holds the stars in space?" "How long do butterflies live?" not to mention, "What do you call that yucky white stuff that grows on your tongue?"

254

They pass most of their days in "learning mode," observing and questioning almost everything. But then, as years go by, most of us seem to give up the quest to learn all that we can about the world around us. It could be that some of us just assume we know plenty enough to make it through our lives without learning stuff we don't have to. Or it could be that we just grow tired and lazy, satisfied with the little we already know because it doesn't require expending any further mental energy.

Whatever the cause, I have come to believe that many of us have sold ourselves short. It is such a shame to stop learning! There are so many wonderful things all around us to explore and discover ... so many things that would make us glad if we could only learn them. But the problem is, we aren't aware of what we don't know. We only know those things we already know. So how can we learn things that we never knew we never knew?

It's really not that hard. We just have to open our eyes and our minds, as we did when we were children, to the wonders around us. There are a million different ways to learn new things every day. Learning is an attitude, a way of living. It's not an artificial, put-on disposition like the one we once saw in a little Inca village in Ecuador. A group of American tourists arrived by boat "to see the Indians." One of those tourists, who was wearing a little white safari outfit complete with a "jungle hat," proceeded to step ashore like Columbus discovering the New World.

"Let's see what these natives have to teach us," I heard him say to his imaginary fan club as he marched toward the village with his jaw stuck up in the air. True learning only comes when genuine interest is mingled with the humility of realizing that we really don't already know it all.

What I am most interested in is our truly wanting to be learners. If we don't care about expanding our horizons, then we will pass by the opportunities the Lord places before us each day. What would happen if children stopped growing prematurely? Can you imagine arriving at, say, 4 feet, 9 inches tall and saying, *Well, that's enough! I've grown all I need to.* Why then, should our minds stop growing before their potential has been reached? Do we really want to be stunted as far as our interest and understanding of God's creation and His workings go?

Once, when our family took a few vacation days at the end of the year, we determined to do things a little differently. We all decided that we wanted to go somewhere and see some things we never had before. So, without any fixed itinerary, we headed up to the Peten. Along the way, we stayed on a river, took a little boat up to the Caribbean coast, and learned from the Garifina culture of Livingston (a town with no roads leading to it). After that, we drove on up to Tikal and stayed in the nature reserve.

We heard jaguars in the jungle at night, howler monkeys at dusk, watched anteaters and spider monkeys and saw many new varieties of trees and birds and other wildlife we had never seen before. Our children, Lindsay and Will, took a "canopy tour" through the trees by strapping on a safety harness and then being lifted up to treetop level and propelling themselves along seven stations throughout the jungle canopy. They had a blast! Lindsay described her adventures to a friend in an email and then chuckled at how bizarre it sounded. We all learned so many new things, and we felt especially grateful to have had the opportunity to experience firsthand such a beautiful area of the world.

What would you like to learn about this year? You don't have to live in Guatemala to find a world of fascination! Wonder is all around us. If we but open our eyes wherever we are, we will discover that there is a whole world of knowledge that we never knew we never knew.

Did you know that some birds fly in their sleep? I recently learned that swifts can fly while actually sleeping! (Talk about your multitasking!) Did you know that the Great Dusky Swift nests behind waterfalls? What a way to bring your little ones into this world! Did you know that sailfish are the fastest swimmers in the ocean, traveling at speeds of up to 68 miles an hour — which is faster than a cheetah can run (a mere 63 mph)? Do you know what the largest mammal on Earth is? (No, it is not your Aunt Eunice!) It is the Blue Whale. Did you know that the horn of a rhino is not really a horn at all? It is made of tightly packed hair-like fibers. Are you familiar with the Mirror Orchid? It has flowers that look very much like little female bees in order to attract male bees to it so that it can spread its pollen.

Did you know that oysters change their sex throughout their lives, living as males sometimes and females at others? (No wonder they look so strange!) Have you ever smelled a Rafflesia plant? Believe it or not, it smells just like rotting flesh! Definitely not one you want to plant among the sweet-smellers of your rose garden!

Did you know that the ancient Mayans developed one of the most perfect calendars mankind has ever produced, and that it has only had one or two errors in the past couple thousand years? Did you know that their calendar was round and not square like ours? And are you familiar with the mystery and beliefs of the ancient Maya concerning the ending of the world's calendar in the year 2012? (Bet you never knew you never knew that!)

And last but not least (or, come to think of it, in this case it probably is least!), the white stuff on your tongue is called bacteria if it is completely normal, or candida or thrush if it is in great excess or if you have recently installed a tongue ring — in which case it is merely a sign from the Lord that you have done a very silly thing to your own tongue!

Oh, there are so many things to learn in this old world!

How is your learning quotient? Are you interested in learning and discovering the wonders of God in our world like a little child, or are you "all grown up" and satisfied that you know all you need to? I hope for your sake that the former condition describes your life today! Think about the mysteries of life that call us to further exploration! It would be so exciting to learn things that we never knew we never knew, don't you think?

What would you most like to explore this year? How will you make sure that you stay a learner when the pressures of work and family make their claims upon you? If you seek to be a learner, ask God, and He will provide the way.

Just as there are millions of things to learn from nature, there is also an eternity of truths to be discovered from God's Word! Are we exploring the Bible each day to learn the truths of God? Why not make this year a year of discovering Bible truths that we never knew we never knew? We would be much better followers of our Lord if our quest for learning from His Word were to be rekindled within us! Won't you join me in these pursuits?

*Lord, please teach us to open our eyes and ears
and our hearts and minds to all the truths You want to teach
us. Permit us to learn from the world around us
just how wonderful You are and how Your handiwork reveals
Your glory. Teach us from your Word Your unfolding plan
for our lives and how to live our lives in Your kingdom.
And may everything that we learn cause us to praise You
more intelligently and love You more dearly.
Have Your way not only in our minds
but in our hearts as well, and may our learning never stop.
We ask it in Jesus' name.
Amen.*

## 11.2
### Turning Life's Sunken Roads into Successes

*And going a little farther he fell on his face and prayed,*
*"My Father, if it be possible, let this cup pass from me;*
*nevertheless, not as I will, but as thou wilt." And he came*
*to the disciples and found them sleeping; and he said to Peter,*
*"So could you not watch with me one hour? Watch and pray*
*that you may not enter into temptation;*
*the spirit indeed is willing, but the flesh is weak."*
– Matthew 26:39–41

THE YEAR WAS 1815, and the place was a little town about 7.5 miles outside Brussels called Waterloo. Napoleon Bonaparte knew that he had a battle to fight, and he had a well-trained army of 73,000 men awaiting his commands.

He knew that he had to face two enemies at once: The Duke of Wellington with the United Kingdom's forces and Gebhard von Blucher with the forces of Prussia. Napoleon knew the approximate lay of the land and understood what he must do to try and divide and conquer his enemies. But oddly enough, all that Napoleon knew didn't matter nearly so much as what he didn't know. That's what made Waterloo his undoing.

The armies met on June 18, following days of hard rains that had left the battleground soggy. Napoleon had only recently returned from exile and was eager to put down his enemies so that his continued rule on the French throne would be secure. He knew that the opposing armies would outnumber his own. As it turned out, his 73,000 men would have to face more than 127,000 men — certainly not the ratio he would have hoped for. Even so, he was confident that his strategy of dividing his men and fighting the battle on two fronts would keep his enemies occupied and contained. Napoleon planned to cut them up and chew them in little pieces — only it didn't quite work out the way he planned.

On the day of the battle, Napoleon and his leaders looked over the beautiful field before them and planned where to position their men. There they made their first crucial mistake. The ground was much soggier and more slippery than they understood. This would cause their horses and armaments to bog down, greatly reducing the force of their attacks.

Another thing that Napoleon's field glasses failed to tell him was that, hidden from view, a sunken road lay in his way. Because he couldn't see it, he didn't prepare for it. According to some, this sunken road, perhaps more than anything else, led to Napoleon's defeat at Waterloo.

Victor Hugo, in his work *Les Miserables*, wrote about the effects this sunken road had on the Battle of Waterloo. According to Hugo, approximately one-third of Napoleon's horsemen fell into this gulch. The horses and their riders were on the move, and by the time those on the front line saw the dropoff, it was too late. Others coming from behind couldn't stop in time and drove the front lines off the embankment and into the sunken road.

Imagine the effect of having so many of your men out of commission. Hugo described the significance of the sunken road like this: "And here the loss of the battle began ... ."

Sunken roads are often the cause of our own defeats. These low points on the battlefields of our lives can cause us to stumble and fall, can't they? We know that we must face battles ... this isn't surprising. We prepare ourselves to have enemies and to be attacked. But there are some things that we just cannot see with our eyes; it is these hidden ditches that can most easily trip us up and make us fall. But if we can't see them, how can we prepare for them?

When Jesus came to face the biggest battle of his life — the agony of the cross — He knew that He couldn't win the battle alone. He fell to His knees and sought His Father's perfect will and His strength. Only through intimate communion with His Father did our Lord find the strength to face the absolute horror of the next hours. Not so with His disciples. ... When Jesus came back from praying, He found His followers asleep! This happened not once, but three times, according to Matthew's Gospel. Three times the disciples closed their eyes and fell asleep on the job, even though Jesus had told them that the hardest times of their lives were about to begin. His orders to them? "Watch and pray that you may not enter into temptation." He reminded them that although the spirit may be willing, the flesh is weak.

What sunken roads lie hidden before you and me as we face the battles of our lives today? I'll bet you don't have a clue as to what all of them are at this point. I don't know either! But I do know this: Jesus told us to stay awake and to watch and pray. Unless we are like Gideon's best troops, who wouldn't even drink without keeping their eyes up and open for dangers (Judg. 7:5), we will be hit broadside by the trials of life. Faith is keeping our eyes open and being watchful. This means that we will be expecting to be in one battle after another. Life is not just one battle; it is an ongoing series of battles that do not end until Jesus calls us home. If we don't expect this, we are foolish about what the Christian life really is!

What happens when we try to stay watchful but know that there are some things that we just cannot see or understand, much less win against? How do we prepare for the sunken roads that will, no doubt, catch us unaware? This is precisely where prayer comes in. We need to face our battles first and foremost through prayer. The truth is that we cannot make it on our own. Only through prayer can we prepare for the sunken roads sure to come our way. Only through a close, intimate walk with God can we be sustained. We cannot win the battle through our own might. "Not by might, nor by power, but by my Spirit, says the Lord of hosts" (Zech. 4:6b).

You and I can't know today all that we will have to face tomorrow (or, to be honest, even later on in this day!) We can plan, we can develop our strategies, and we can prepare in many ways for facing our battles. But only an intimate communication with God will give us the strength and wisdom we need to turn our sunken roads into successes!

So as we, like Napoleon, hold up our field glasses and scout the battlefields ahead, let us not make the mistake of assuming we can handle everything on our own. Let us look from one side of the field to the other, and let us make our plans accordingly, but, while we are looking and planning, let us also be in constant prayer, asking God to direct us so that we might not be overcome by any sunken roads.

Prayer is the true path to victory!

# 11.3
## Buried Treasure
🌿

*"The kingdom of heaven is like treasure hidden in a field,
which a man found and covered up; then in his joy he goes and sells
all that he has and buys that field...."*
– Matthew 13:44

I'VE ALWAYS LOVED THE PARABLE ABOVE. Jesus explains one of the mysteries of the universe in a down-to-earth, simple way that all of us can understand. We find on the surface of this story a man who manages to stumble upon the greatest discovery of his life. Once he has found the treasure of treasures, what does he do? He carefully covers it back up ... until he is able return to it a little later. I can just imagine his giddiness as he rushes around taking inventory of all he owns and measuring his life's worth against that extraordinary treasure buried out in the field. With joy he sells all that he has and buys that field so that the treasure can be his.

Of course, Jesus in this parable is not talking only about buying and selling and making a profit. He is talking about discovering what the most important things in life are, and then what we should do once we learn how to obtain them. That treasure is our personal salvation, a sense of purpose and meaning in this world, and the merging of our lives with the kingdom of God.

In Tajumulco Mam, the heart-language of our people group, there is no adequate expression for the "kingdom of God." The closest equivalent is something like "where we are under the authority of God." It has more to do with who is in charge of our lives than it does with a physical location. It is simply where God rules and where we really experience living.

There is one more thing. There remains a nagging question before us. It is the old, old question of what to keep and what to throw away. Is what we have more valuable than God having His way in and through us? Of course not! Then why do we keep hanging onto things that we have gained through the years? Could it be that we are afraid to let go — that although we know how temporary our holdings are, we still prefer to hold onto our security rather than trust God?

If we, like the wise man in the parable, were to inventory all that we have and weigh it against giving ourselves over totally to God's will, what things would we need to let go of? Would it be our pride, our comfort, our pleasures? Our lack of forgiveness to others for past hurts or wounds? Our fears and self-doubts? Or ambitions for a good life in the present and future?

Whatever we choose to hold onto that keeps us from being totally sold out to God is not worth it. If we would but let go of our money, our possessions, our schedules and all those other weights that we have used as excuses for not giving ourselves over to the will of God, we would discover a joy deeper than we have ever known. What He has for us is infinitely better than what we have gained for ourselves.

How about a deal? (Or as my grandfather used to say, "How you trade?") Your junk for His treasure. Everything that you have for everything that He has. That's what He is offering. Hurry! Take it quickly because, like all good deals, this is a limited-time offer. It's a trade that none of us will ever regret!

## 11.4
## The Issue of Abandonment

*[Elijah] said, "I have been very jealous for the Lord,*
*the God of hosts; for the people of Israel have forsaken*
*thy covenant, thrown down thy altars and slain thy prophets*
*with the sword; and I, even I only, am left;*
*and they seek my life, to take it away."*
– 1 Kings 19:10

*After this many of his disciples drew back and no longer*
*went about with him. Jesus said to the twelve,*
*"Do you also wish to go away?"*
– John 6:66–67

Do you ever feel small, alone or abandoned? Most of us do at some time or another. Psychologists tell us that we all struggle between two extremes: the fear of absorption and the fear of abandonment. On the one hand, we don't want to be paid so much attention that we lose our identity, our individualism or our sense of self (e.g., those who struggle with an overly possessive parent who makes every decision for an adult child). On the other hand, we don't want to be left alone or abandoned, either. Which extreme is worse? I'll let you decide. To me, both are pretty bad.

In the movie "O Brother, Where Art Thou?", three men break away from their chain gang in order to recover a treasure

267

before it is submerged in the lake that will be created by a new dam. One of the characters, Pete, is captured by police. They tie him up and put a noose around his neck as they try to force him to reveal what he knows about his fellow escapees.

"Pete, it seems that your friends have all abandoned you!" he is told. The combination of a noose around his neck and the abandonment of his friends is too much to bear. Pete tells all. Abandonment can be a pretty strong force to deal with! (But so can a rope around your neck!)

For many of God's servants through the ages, abandonment has been a real issue. Elijah had shown extraordinary courage for the Lord, but even so, he came to feel that he was all alone (although he really wasn't). "And I, even I only, am left ..." he complained. Others who should have been standing alongside Elijah had abandoned their faith and had abandoned him. He felt alone. So he responded by hiding in a cave feeling sorry for himself. Many of us have been there too, haven't we?

We can be (or feel) abandoned in many different ways. Some children feel abandoned because of instability at home during their early years. Divorce breaks up the family and causes a child (and the parents also) to be lost. Frequent moving can make a person feel that he or she is alone and that there is no one who can be counted upon.

Wayne E. Oates, one of my favorite professors in seminary and perhaps the best pastoral care professor/counselor/author that Southern Baptists have ever produced, grew up on a mill hill in Greenville, South Carolina. His father abandoned him, his mother, and his brothers and sisters when Wayne was very small. As he struggled with the poverty and low self-esteem that comes from abandonment, Wayne knew some tough times. He was fortunate, though, to be blessed with people in his life who believed in the Lord and knew that He had special plans for Wayne.

By grace, he was lifted out of his situation, educated and given an opportunity to use the pain of his early childhood to relate to others who were hurting. The key to his success, really, was discovering that although his earthly father had abandoned him and his family, there was a heavenly Father who had not — and would never do so! This understanding revolutionized his life and gave him a foundation from which to help others in pain find a faith in God that would see them through as well.

The apostle Paul knew what it was like to be abandoned. He was despised and rejected by the Jews because of his stand for Jesus. During one missionary journey, he was abandoned by John Mark. He was laughed at by those who were his equals in education and training.

Some of you may be reading these words on a college campus, and you feel alone there in your stand for Him, just as Paul was. In prison, Paul was forgotten by many who should have supported him. I know that some of you are reading these words from prison cells as well, and that you may feel totally abandoned and forgotten. Some of you are facing illnesses and are spending your days and nights in hospitals, keeping a lonely watch and praying for deliverance and a restoration of health for loved ones. The issue of abandonment is a common theme for so many across our world.

Even our Lord felt the sting of abandonment often during his earthly ministry. He was rejected by many who knew Him only as the son of a small-town carpenter. He was despised by those in power because He spoke the truth. He was rejected and targeted as being too radical by the church of His day. Throughout His ministry He was surrounded by narrow-minded, shortsighted people who didn't want to know the truth; they only wanted Him to agree with their version of it. His followers praised Him one day and deserted Him the next. At one point, so many were leaving Him that He turned and asked even the twelve who knew Him most intimately, "Do you also wish to go away?"

In the hours leading up to the cross, His disciples could not even stay awake with Him. When He most needed the company of His supporters, He found Himself utterly alone, humanly speaking. And while He hung because of our sins upon the cross in those final hours, He was abandoned even by God for a short while. Jesus knows what it is to be abandoned.

Many servants of God feel abandoned because they must stand alone at times. Perhaps the church or organization where you serve has little vision, leaving you with people who are hard to work with. Perhaps you are the only Christian where you work and you feel laughed at, alone and forgotten much of the time. Maybe you have taken a stand, and others around you have distanced themselves and taken a different stance, leaving you to feel as if you're standing alone for the truth. It can be hard, can't it? Sometimes we, like Elijah, can feel abandoned.

How are things where you serve? Do you enjoy the support of others? If so, thank God for it. If you do not have that support — if instead you feel abandoned and alone, know this: Even though it's hard to stand alone and be a witness for the truth, you can endure it! God has promised not to burden us with more than we can bear. Perhaps we would not be overly dramatic to believe that God allows us to be in some situations because we can bear it while others in that situation might not have been able to. By ourselves, we are weak. But if we stand for Him and for His kingdom's purposes, we will never really stand alone. He will stand with us!

If you are down or lonely this week, why not read again Romans Chapter 8 and be reminded that, even if the whole world should turn against us, He will never desert us! Never! No matter where we are (workplace, church, mission field, hospital, university campus, prison, in our own home, or anyplace else) and no matter what we might be facing, He will be there with us! And He will continue to stand with us until the end . . . .

Count on it!

# 11.5
## The Issue of Absorption

*But when Herod's birthday came, the daughter of Herodias danced
before the company, and pleased Herod, so that he promised
with an oath to give her whatever she might ask.
Prompted by her mother, she said, "Give me the head
of John the Baptist here on a platter."*
...
*[Herod] sent and had John beheaded in the prison,
and his head was brought on a platter and given to the girl,
and she brought it to her mother.*
– Matthew 14:6–8; 10–11

---

*Another of his disciples said to him, "Lord, let me first go
and bury my father." But Jesus said to him, "Follow me
and leave the dead to bury their own dead."*
– Matthew 8: 21–22

WE HAVE SAID THAT ABANDONMENT is one extreme of two issues that face so many of God's people. The other extreme is that of absorption. For our purposes, let us say that absorption refers to a pull by someone else who seeks to control us and cause us to be and act as he or she wishes. Absorption is usually achieved to our own detriment.

Why am I talking about concepts that some may consider psychological drivel? I am talking about them because they affect so many of us, and we need to be aware of them so that our lives and the lives of those we love are not damaged by them. Abandonment and absorption are like the two black dogs that the character Christian encountered and had to walk between in *The Pilgrim's Progress*. If we get too close to either abandonment or absorption, we will be devoured.

Still lost? Let me give you an example of what I am talking about. A lady I know was so controlled by her mother that her marriage broke apart. There were many other issues (there always are), but absorption was a primary problem. When the lady had children, her mother told her exactly what she could and could not do to raise them. She wanted to be included in almost every activity that her daughter and her family ever had.

When her husband was offered a very good job in another town a few hours away, her mother locked herself in a room and refused to come out until her "baby girl" came to her senses and returned home. The daughter cried and cried and forced her husband to quit his job and move back to her hometown because "Mama just can't bear to be apart from us." Mama did not want to go live with them. She wanted them to come back and live in her neighborhood. Mama controlled everything about her daughter's life even after she was married with a family of her own. Even after the daughter's divorce, she has never been able to bring herself to do anything that did not "please Mama." Needless to say, she has never really been happy.

Another man was raised by a mother who, when he was in grade school, begged him to stay home and keep her company rather than go to school. As he grew into his teenage years, she would at times become furious with him because he wasn't popular enough to provide her with good "bragging stories" to

273

share with her sisters and friends. In her mind, his purpose in life was to serve her needs. He was there for her fulfillment. As he chose his profession, married and moved away, she constantly harassed him and tried to coax him into returning to the town where she lived so that he could be "next door to Mama." She had no interest in visiting him where he lived and seeing his life as he and his family had made it. She only wanted him to do what she wanted him to do in the place that she chose. Needless to say, this man also struggled with guilt for "disappointing Mama."

Just as we shouldn't allow others to absorb us, we also shouldn't practice self-absorption. Perhaps this — allowing our own ego to reign supreme — is the most common and dangerous form of absorption. Those who are self-absorbed believe they should do whatever makes them happiest. They expect spouses and children, friends and family, and any who enter their inner circle to put them and their desires first.

"It's my life and I can do whatever I want!" we may think. Maybe we can do whatever we want, but it is not "our life." We are not our own; we have been bought with a price. We all have an appointment one day to give an account of our lives and to explain what we did with what He gave us. Self-absorption on that day will be a very sorry excuse indeed for not having used our lives to serve God!

Absorption can attack from many sides. Although absorption problems often come from our own selves or from a parent, they can also come from close friends, other relatives, or even from our boss or company where we work. For so many people, there are voices wanting to control them and to make their decisions for them. And what is wrong with someone else making our decisions for us? Just this: our God is a jealous God, and He will not tolerate anyone else — not us, not our best friend, not our employer, and not even Mama — to take the role of a god in our lives. We are commanded to listen first and foremost to His instructions. His will is the only one that we must be sure to follow. Please do not misunderstand me and think that I am saying that loving and honoring our mothers and our fathers is not important. It certainly is! I am just saying that no one should be allowed to rule our lives except God. Only He can fill the top spot of command for all our decision making.

I am convinced that there are many people who are not on the mission field, in Christian vocations, or wherever and in whatever capacity He may lead because doing so would "break Mama's heart" if they moved that far away. Many stay home and choose another life because they do not want to disappoint someone they care about. However, how do they justify hurting the one — God Himself — about whom they should care the most?

On the other hand, I also know of a case in which a husband forced his wife to go to the mission field. She didn't want to go and felt no sense of call whatsoever to do so. She went simply because she did not want to disappoint her husband. She and her family, of course, eventually resigned and came home. As much as her husband would have liked to have played god in her life, that spot was not open to him.

Why do we do take steps that we know are wrong for us merely because we don't want to disappoint somebody? When the daughter of Herodias danced before Herod, I am quite sure that her heart's desire was not to be given a man's head on a platter. She asked for it only because Mama wanted it that way.

Absorption again. We do not know the exact age of the daughter, but if she was old enough to delight a crowd of men, she was old enough to think for herself. Because she listened to Mama, she made the wrong move, asked for the wrong thing, and caused great harm.

When one man attempted to beg off from following Jesus in Matthew 8, Jesus told him to let the dead bury their own! Does that sound harsh? How could Jesus have been so heartless? Some have suggested that perhaps his father was not even dead yet and that he was talking about going back to Daddy and being close to him in his old age instead of following Jesus. Whatever the case, Jesus laid down the rules: We are to follow God's leadership before anyone else's desires. Anyone else's plan for us that disagrees with God's will for us will just lead us away from what we need to be doing.

What absorption forces are present in your life? Is your voice louder than God's? Is it the voice of Mama or Daddy? Is it a close friend or relative? Is it your employer?

Whenever outside forces try to control how we think, act and spend our lives, we need to be very careful. We should always pray, asking that, "Thy kingdom come. Thy will be done...." Our goal is to be absorbed into His will, is it not? Jesus said that we are to pay tribute to whom tribute is due and we are to respect, love and listen to the advice of those whom we care very much about. But God's will, as best as we can understand it, should always be the deciding voice in any decision we ever make.

If you have struggled in your past with a controlling voice that compelled you to move in directions apart from God's will in your life, or if you today are under pressure to be something that you are not meant to be because you do not want to disappoint someone close to you, God still offers us the grace and the help to change. Even though some may not understand it, our best hope of happiness and fulfillment is being in the center of God's will for us — not necessarily being in the center of anyone else's will for us.

Whose will are you living out today? Your own? Someone else's who had their own plans for you? Or are you daily living out God's best plans for you? I suggest that we search our hearts and make sure that we seek with all our might to live out God's will as best as we can discern it — whether those who may seek to absorb us are happy with that decision or not!

# CHAPTER TWELVE

# Moving Toward an Authentic Faith

## 12.1
## Surviving Life's Quicksand

*...Save me, O God! For the waters have come up to my neck.
I sink in deep mire, where there is no foothold ....*
– Psalm 69:1–2

*The steps of a man are from the Lord and he establishes him
in whose way he delights ....*
– Psalm 37:23

Ever HAD A CLOSE ENCOUNTER with quicksand? Not the made-for-movies variety, but the real stuff? I have to confess that we have. (I know, I know. You're probably thinking, *Stone, you've led such a weird life that we're not surprised at anything!*) Even so, experiences (even bad ones) can be blessings if we learn from them.

From 1979 to 1981 we served in the eastern jungle of Ecuador as journeymen doing evangelism and medical work. Lily's medical ministry there led us to meet a couple named Pablo and Olga, who lived out in the jungle near a village called Chiritza. They lived out — way out!

We had driven past their house before and noted that it sat far off the road and was surrounded by a bog. Therefore we were somewhat dubious when Lily received a call for help from them one day. Olga was pregnant and sick, and we were told that she could not make it to the road in order to come see us. (Soon we were to find out why ... .) Lily was asked to go in to treat her.

We asked one of our neighbors with whom we often worked to go in with us. "No, Sister!" he replied to Lily. "I can't go back in there. Last time I went, I fell in and nearly died in the quicksand! I will lend you my boots, though."

When we got to the entrance to their property, we were pretty frightened at what we found. The path from the road to their house consisted of about six lengths of thick bamboo poles on the right side, secured end to end by bits of dry land. Another six poles on the other side led back out. We were immediately shaken when we realized that there was just one pole (not two!) to walk over on each side! Even worse, below the poles was a nasty-looking bog that contained spots of quicksand. Making matters even trickier was the fact that we had to take in Lily's leather medical bag, which weighed around 50 pounds. (Guess who got to carry that?)

Off we went, walking sideways across the poles, trying to keep our balance and praying fervently that we would not fall in. I must say that we made it only by God's grace. We got there and back, and Lily was able to help nurse Olga back to health.

I have been thinking a lot lately about how important balance is in life. Life is really a series of walks across short poles with a lot of mire below that we can fall into if we're not careful. When we are tilted too far to the right or to the left, we struggle to keep our footing. We get so confused about who we are as we attempt to walk between our cultural mindset and the call of Christ to follow straight behind Him.

We hear a great many voices calling to us to follow. The world's business models that call for efficiency are laid across

God's call to put our focus on people and on ministering to them in Christ's name. We are pulled to extremes — first this way and then another. At times, despite our very best efforts, we all fall down. How do we keep our balance when the way is so tenuous?

At times the Psalmist also found himself sinking in the mire "where there is no foothold." He was well aware of the consequences of a life that tilts too far. He concludes that, although it isn't easy, there is no other way to make it through life than to let God order our feet. Only in the Lord do we find the proper balance to stay on the poles. We must not listen to the voices of others around us who would cause us to lean too far. We must close our eyes and focus on only His voice. Only by His daily leading do we avoid falling into the mire. Only by His grace can we stay in God's will.

Whenever we find that we have tilted and fallen, instead of despairing, we would do well to heed the old straightforward formula for success: "When you fall down — get up!"

In the end, the Christian walk is about getting back up, steadying our feet on His path and staying the course until the journey is ended. In Him, not only do we "live and move and have our being," but we find balance that keeps us on the path. One step at a time, with sweat on our brows and the Son in our eyes, we press on. May we walk the walk today with holy conviction, with integrity and uprightness of heart, and with the balance that comes only from Him. Only a few more poles to walk and we will be there!

Walk on!

## 12.2
## Taking the Risk

*...And the high priest questioned them, saying,*
*"We strictly charged you not to teach in this name, yet here you*
*have filled Jerusalem with your teaching and you intend*
*to bring this man's blood upon us." But Peter and the apostles*
*answered, "We must obey God rather than men."...*
– Acts 5:27b–29

LIVING INVOLVES TAKING RISKS. Inside of most of us, however, there is an inner voice that cautions us to "play it safe."

"Don't rock the boat," we're warned. "Go along to get along." We often find ourselves avoiding trouble and taking the path of least resistance in order to be well thought of by our employers, peers and others whose opinions we value. Even so, there are times when all of us must decide whether to duck our heads and play it safe or to take the risks involved in what we know in our hearts to be right. This is our ongoing conflict, isn't it?

I have mentioned my brother Steve in other stories. Steve too is in the family business; we're both out to change the world! He has been a Baptist pastor in South Carolina for many years. One evening a few years ago, Steve wearily made his way to the hospital to visit one of his church members who would be having surgery the next day. It was late in the evening, but Steve felt he needed to check on his sick friend and church member. As Steve came down the hallway searching for the right room, he noticed an older man across the hall staring at him. He nodded to the man, then went in to visit his church member. He had a good visit talking, listening and praying with his friend, and, when it was time to leave, he was really tired and ready to get back home.

Coming out of the room, Steve thought again of the man across the hall. He didn't know him, had never seen him before, but he decided on the spur of the moment to go and visit the man. He had no idea if his visit would be welcomed.

The gentleman was still awake and graciously received Steve into his room. Steve introduced himself, and, after a little bit, began to share his faith in Christ. The man listened, and before the conversation was over, he told Steve that he was ready to believe in the Lord and had been waiting for someone to come and explain it all to him. He received Christ as his Lord that night from his sick bed. Steve was thrilled!

The next day Steve made his way back to the hospital to be with his church member after his surgery. He had come through just fine. After a short visit with him, Steve thought he might just pop over and see the new believer across the hall.

As he walked into the room, he discovered the bed was empty. Steve asked a nurse where he could find the gentleman. The nurse looked at him and said, "I'm sorry. He passed away last night ... died peacefully in his sleep."

One and only one opportunity had existed for Steve to share with the man about the love of God and His offer of salvation through Jesus. What if he had not taken the risk and visited a stranger on a late-night hospital ward? Those few minutes of risk that my brother took made a difference for all of eternity in the soul of that man. Sharing the gospel with others can be a risky proposition, but Steve will never regret taking the risk that night.

Peter and the apostles took a very big and very real risk in proclaiming their faith in the risen Lord Jesus when they had been ordered not to. Witnessing must have been very uncomfortable in their circumstances. Their very lives were in danger. Yet they took the risk for the sake of making the kingdom of God a reality among so many who had never heard. What if they had not taken the risk? Perhaps we would never have had the opportunity to hear the gospel!

What is God calling us to risk for Him today? Risk is uncomfortable and sometimes downright scary. We face possible rejection, being thought of as fools, and being written off by others. Yet what will we lose if we do not take the risks God opens before us?

Disobeying God costs much more than it ever gains anyone. Not taking the risk of sharing Christ with a world of lost and dying persons means, in some cases, no more opportunities to hear ... to believe ... to be saved from eternal death.

We must take risks if we are to be faithful to God.

## 12.3
### Tales From a Blackberry Picker
🌿

*Put in the sickle, for the harvest is ripe... .*
– Joel 3:13

*... "The harvest is plentiful, but the laborers are few;*
*pray therefore the Lord of the harvest*
*to send out laborers into the harvest."*
– Matthew 9:37–38

I LOVE SUMMERTIME! It's my favorite season of the year, for several reasons. For one thing, I really enjoy the warm weather. Walking through the woods, swimming in the lake, going to the beach, and being outside are very enjoyable experiences for me. I love the shades of green, the flowers, and the lushness of the trees. Summer aromas, the long days and delightful evenings spent with family and close friends make summer the ideal season. As the old line from the musical "Porgy and Bess" puts it, "Summertime/And the livin' is easy." Yep, summer works for me.

One of the special summer joys for me is picking blackberries. In late June and early July, South Carolina blackberries are at their peak, just ripe for the picking. I looked around the other day and found blackberries growing in three different spots in the woods near our little trailer. While leaning over the vines to take a closer look, I noticed that there were blackberries in all stages of ripeness; some were still red, while others were perfectly ripe. Some were very small. Others were medium-sized, and still others were huge! I tasted some of them and found that some were still a bit sour, even though they were totally ripe. Others were as sweet as could be and tasted delicious.

As I bent over to pick the ripest ones, I noticed that some were much easier to reach than other ones. Some were hidden behind other vines and were not very visible until you got close. And as I picked a handful at a time, a few dropped to the ground. I was able to retrieve some, but others were lost in the undergrowth.

There were so many blackberries that I realized I couldn't harvest them all by myself. Some of them were already perishing on the vines because I didn't get to them soon enough. I went to my family and asked for their help, and the four of us went together with a big bowl to pick for a while. It's amazing how much faster the picking goes when you don't try to do it all by yourself!

Picking blackberries isn't always easy. The sun gets pretty hot. The briars on the vines prick and sometimes cause you to bleed a little. You must be ever mindful to watch out for snakes hiding in the thickets! It's hard work, and you usually get all hot and sweaty. Overripe specimens stain your hands with blackberry juice. Aside from that, it takes a bit of time to go to where blackberries grow and more time to pick them. Yes, there are several reasons why most people don't go out to pick blackberries these days. After all, you can buy frozen blackberries, and it's a lot easier to let others do the picking. It's easier still to just take it for granted that there will always be blackberries harvested from somewhere. Nevertheless, I can think of three good reasons to go picking:

1. There is a plentiful, ripe harvest out there just waiting for us to claim it.
2. There is nothing in the world like a blackberry pie when you get a whole bunch of them together!
3. The final product is wonderful and worth all the effort! The briar wounds and the sweat are soon forgotten when you get to enjoy a bowl of them (as I am doing as I write this!).

Yes, siree ... I am a committed blackberry picker! I don't ever want to stop picking them or to miss out on the wonderful foods that they can become.

You know, whenever I pick blackberries, I am reminded of an even greater harvest out there waiting for us. Matthew 9 reminds us of a harvest of souls ripe for the picking! And when people's lives are not harvested, what's lost are the eternal souls of men and women and boys and girls ... people who are forever separated from the God who loves them so!

All around the world, there are people of different colors, from different cultures and with different languages who all are growing in God's garden here on this Earth. As it is with blackberries, we are able to harvest even where we did not plant. The Holy Spirit is present throughout the Earth, placing conviction of sin and emptiness in human hearts that can only be filled by God's presence in their lives.

I don't think we can truly comprehend the tragedy of billions of human souls slipping into eternity without Jesus Christ as their Lord and Savior. I don't think we can even imagine the atrocity of such a great harvest rotting on the vines because we did not take the time to gather in the ripe fruit!

The harvest of the whole world is laid out before us. How will we respond? Will we shrink back because it isn't convenient or because we'll get messy, cut, hot and bothered? Will we assume that others will do the job? Instead of getting dirty in the work of the harvest, will we let the stains on our hands be the blood of those with whom we didn't share our witness of what Jesus has done in our lives?

In Central America 70 different language/dialect groups need to hear the gospel of our Lord. There are thousands more people groups around the planet who also need to know the Lord. Indeed, there are opportunities all around us, be it in the cul-de-sacs of our communities or in a little village on the other side of the world. Literally, we must go and make disciples of all peoples everywhere. Evangelism must take place in communities all around us through home missions and international missions. It is not a matter of either-or; it is a mandate of both. The lost are all around us. The question is: What do we intend to do about it?

As much as I'd like for you to get the opportunity to pick some blackberries this summer, even more I hope that you get to be a part of the great harvest of souls that is ripe for the picking if we will only be faithful in sharing the glorious news of the gospel of Jesus Christ! Yes, involvement in the lives of lost friends is messy and costly — but the value of winning even one soul is eternal and priceless!

Happy picking!

# 12.4
## A Continual Feast

*And God saw everything that he had made,*
*and behold, it was very good.*
– Genesis 1:31a

---

*All the days of the afflicted are evil,*
*but a cheerful heart has a continual feast.*
– Proverbs 15:15

Oɴᴇ ᴏꜰ ᴛʜᴇ ᴍᴏꜱᴛ ᴄᴏʟᴏʀꜰᴜʟ collections of writings ever gathered together in a book was penned by Ernest Hemingway and is called *A Moveable Feast*. In this book, Hemingway gives the reader a bird's-eye view of what it is like to be a young writer living in Paris in the 1920s, hobnobbing with the likes of James Joyce, Ezra Pound and F. Scott Fitzgerald. His descriptions of the people, the sights, sounds and the meals enjoyed there remain timeless and unforgettable.

To Hemingway, Paris was a moveable feast to be enjoyed by the rich and the poor, the young and the old. Just reading the book makes one feel alive and caught up in the great adventure that we call living.

Life is intended by God to be a great adventure! It is especially so for Christians who understand that we are just getting started with a life that will count for God's eternal purpose and one that will ultimately end in glorious, exciting victory! We can't lose!

Have you ever wondered, then, why Christians aren't happier? We should be the most joyful people on the planet! Instead, many of us seem to live like a verse from a John Mellencamp song: "Oh yeah/Life goes on long after the thrill of livin' is gone." Often, we are just too serious for our own good. Maybe, as Oscar Hammerstein wrote in "Ol' Man River," we're "tired of livin'" and "skeered of dyin'."

Now, I know very well that life is full of heartache and sadness. There is sin, sickness, suffering and injustice at every corner. But not all of life is that way! There is also the goodness of God and the blessings of making a feast out of enjoying a creation that God called into being and then pronounced as good.

In my opinion, we sometimes inaccurately use the word "secular" to mean anything that takes place outside a church building, implying that this is somehow less than appropriate for the believer. Where did we ever come up with that? Not from the Scriptures!

When God created all the beautiful things in our world, He proclaimed that they were "very good." We should never forget that. Some of our quasi-evangelical groups here in Guatemala call on their members to reject sports, parties, laughing out loud and anything else that is not very serious. By adopting this mindset, we can find ourselves hesitant to breathe "secular air" or to listen to "secular birds" singing in the trees or to smell the secular Sweet-Breath-of-Spring that grows under the oak trees in the summertime. Thinking and acting this way can get just plain ridiculous!

Please don't misunderstand ... the Scriptures teach us that anything tainted with sin is corrupted and therefore to be avoided. But why should we be willing to ignore so many wonderful things in God's world that are not tainted and are still to be enjoyed and celebrated? It is my belief that God calls us to reject sin in all its forms. I also believe, though, that we should do more celebrating and rejoicing in the gift of life that we have been given. We should live deliberately and uproariously. We ought to laugh more, notice more landscapes, smell more flowers, spend more time listening to music and talking with close friends. We ought to be less serious — especially about ourselves!

The good news for today is that God is God — and we are not! The One who made the green, rolling hills and who put fish in the streams wants us to live life to the fullest and to rejoice in His good creation. What a shame it would be not to enjoy it because we are too busy being serious and trying to appear godly by eschewing activities that resemble play and fun. Why do we need to try to be more serious than God all the time? Somehow many of us have gotten it all so wrong — so terribly wrong!

The writer of Proverbs 15 tells us that, although sin brings affliction and causes pain and sorrow in our lives (anything that is against His will is wrong and should be avoided like the plague!), there is still so much those who seek to faithfully serve Him should be enjoying. God puts some things before us just to make us glad and cheerful.

Sadly, we sometimes fail to take notice. As the saying goes, "Everyone who lives, dies, but not everyone who dies has really lived." I don't want to rush through life so full of myself that I fail to experience the wonders God Himself has provided me.

For those with a cheerful heart, life can be a "continual feast." And as we are also told, "A glad heart makes a cheerful countenance ..." (Prov. 15:13).

Is your heart glad today? Are you able to enjoy the continual feast of life in God's service, or are you on a hunger strike? Jesus came to take us away from the heartache of sin and to allow us to live the abundant life. A life full of gladness and cheer. A life where we can celebrate the blessings of being alive in a world that He designed just for us! He invites us not to merely go through life but to really live it by taking in the beauty of all that lies along our way while we serve Him. As Max Lucado once said, "Your goal is not to live long; it is to live."

How about you? Are you enjoying the feast, or has it all become a drudging chore? Oh, I know it's hard to shut out the seriousness of life, but could we not just every now and again take time to enjoy the feast of life and be happy — deliriously happy? Isn't it time we started proclaiming to a lost world that in Jesus we can all come to the table with cheerful hearts?

Others may want to be like the Pharisees, so serious about everything, giving up laughter and surrendering a cheerful heart, but not me. I'm not willing to pass up the continual feast of enjoying God's goodness. I want to live life to the fullest. What, after all, is there to prevent us from really celebrating those things that God has offered you and me to make us glad? What would happen if we decided to be happy — so happy that those around us who are caught up in sin would sit up and seriously wonder what they're missing? I think they too would wish to come to the feast, the continual feast of abundant life in Jesus Christ ... .

I don't know about you, but for me, life is just too short to be serious all the time. The Lord has not put blinders on our eyes or sacks over our mouths as though we were dumb animals in a field. We have somehow done that to ourselves. While rejecting all the things that threaten to lead us away from God, we shouldn't forget to embrace all the goodness of God in this life here on Earth. That which is good, that which is light, fun, humorous and which makes us laugh is to be embraced. I want to smell the roses, to enjoy oysters-on-the-half-shell and to run and laugh like a kid on his first day of summer vacation. I want others to see in us a life that is lived to the fullest and one that is celebrated with cheerful hearts.

I want people to long for whatever is making us so happy. When life is over for us here on this Earth, I want others to remember us and say, "They saw life in God's service as a continual feast!" That is what I wish.

While you are thinking about it all, would you mind passing me more of those steamed oysters, the rolls and the butter … and maybe one more piece of that cherry cobbler? (Thank you, Jesus!)

# 12.5
## Living Next Door to Jesus

*"This I command you, to love one another."*
– John 15:17

*"You have heard it was said, 'You shall love your neighbor*
*and hate your enemy.' But I say to you, Love your enemies and pray*
*for those who persecute you, so that you may be sons of your Father*
*who is in heaven; for he makes his sun rise on the evil*
*and on the good, and sends rain on the just and on the unjust.*
*For if you love those who love you, what reward have you?*
*Do not even the tax collectors do the same? And if you salute only*
*your brethren, what more are you doing than others?*
*Do not even the Gentiles do the same?"*
– Matthew 5:43–47

SEVERAL YEARS AGO A MISSIONARY colleague named Don was
serving up in the northern part of Guatemala. Don is an humble,
sensitive, loving and very humorous man. The brothers and our
fellow missionaries loved him dearly. You couldn't help but do
so. He radiated a Christ-likeness in all that he did.

One day, however, a disagreement developed between Don
and another man. Things were heating up when the man
stormed down the road on his way to Don's house. "I'm going
to see Don and give him a piece of my mind!" he told Mike, a
fellow missionary. "We're going to settle this once and for all!"

Mike saw this same man a little later as he was leaving Don's house. "Did you get everything worked out?" Mike asked.

The other man said, "I lit into him and really let him have it! But do you know what he did? Don apologized and told me, 'Brother I have wronged you, and I humbly ask you to forgive me. I didn't mean to do anything against you. I'm so sorry!'"

Mike then asked this man if Don's apology made him feel better.

"No, it didn't!" he replied, although all the anger and hot air seemed to have drained out of him. "Living next door to Don is just like living next door to Jesus!" With that, he turned and made his way back home.

I have chuckled about this story many times, and it makes me think. What would the world be like if we all had the love, humility and desire for peace that Don had? What kind of people and Christians would we be if we were more like Don? And if all true Christians were more that way, what would our world be like if everyone had the opportunity to "live next door to Jesus" by living next door to His people?

Have you read any of the disturbing reports about the state of health of Christian churches in the United States lately? Almost everyone has read of the many scandals involving ministers. Some time ago I read another article that made me sad. A little girl had asked her church if she could take the Lord's Supper with communion bread that contained no wheat because she has a disease that makes her violently ill when she eats any wheat product. The response from her church was that rules were rules and she could either take the wheat wafer during the Lord's Supper — or not. How do you suppose the Lord feels about this?

In another situation, some recovering alcoholics asked their church (which uses real wine in its communion tradition) if they could receive grape juice instead of wine. They got the same response as the little girl with the wheat allergy: take it or leave it because, regardless of their need, the rules are the rules.

And keeping the rules is what it's all about, right?

Some recent studies have indicated a decline in church-goers in the United States. There are many factors involved in this drop. One is that fewer people raised in Christian homes remain active in church when they become adults. This really concerns me!

We can make whatever excuses we like, but the sad fact is that we are failing to pass on our faith in the Lord to others — even to those who grow up in our own homes. We have emphasized church attendance and have offered Sunday schools, youth groups, revivals, Bible studies and discipleship programs galore for all age groups, and yet we still see a decline. How can this be?

Can it be that we, despite all our activities and sermons, have fallen short on the one thing that is the most important of all — love? We have tried to preach the gospel, we have emphasized a right relationship with Christ, and we have taught doctrines and stressed walking the straight and narrow. But I wonder how we measure up when it comes to communicating and individually living out the love of Christ to those all around us? Could it be that those who are observing us realize before we do that we are much too long on sermons and far too short on love?

The real truth of the matter is that many of us are so broken inside that we give a negative witness to those around us instead of a positive one. We are so bent on others keeping all the rules that we ourselves can not keep that we forget about being salt and light and about showing Christ's love to the world around us. I wonder how many unbelievers (if any) would say, "I have the opportunity to live next door to Jesus by living next door to [insert your own name here]." It's truly a scary thought, isn't it?

Where is the love that is supposed to identify us as Christians? Remember the old song from the '60s: "And they'll know we are Christians by our love, by our love/They will know we are Christians by our love"? Are we identified by love as Matthew 5 teaches us? Or are we primarily characterized by other traits?

Yes, I know that most true Christians are trying to do the best they can to live out their daily lives and make a difference for God. But I can't help but wonder if maybe we have put our quest for genuine love on the back burner ... behind keeping the laws and being on time for all our meetings at church. How easily we forget the importance of 1 Corinthians 13! (If you haven't read that chapter lately, do so today.) Keeping laws doesn't mean much if it doesn't proceed from a heart of love.

What we need is a heart that will attract others not by condemnation but by genuine agape-like acceptance, mercy, grace and love ... a radiating love that penetrates the heart of others and makes them want to have what we have. I am afraid that I fall way short on this. How about you?

How are our hearts today? Do we love each other in the family of faith? Do we love non-Christians — really? And do they know it by the way we relate to them? It bears repeating: Would they ever say that being near us is like living next door to Jesus? Just think how wonderful the world would be if everyone could say that!

May the love of Jesus take us over and change everything in our lives. And may those around us notice the difference!

How to order more copies of
# What if Everyone Lived Next Door to Jesus?
## by Gary Stone

CALL: 1-800-747-0738
FAX: 1-888-252-3022
Email: orders@hannibalbooks.com
Write: Hannibal Books
P.O. Box 461592
Garland, Texas 75046
Visit: www.hannibalbooks.com

Number of copies of *What if Everyone Lived Next Door to Jesus?*:___

Multiply total number of copies: ____ by $19.95 =

Total cost of books: $_____

Add $3 for postage and handling for the first book plus 50 cents for each additional book in the order.

Shipping total: $_____

Texas residents add 8.25% sales tax: $_____

Total order: $_____

Number on enclosed check _____

Credit card # _____ Exp. date_____
(Visa, MasterCard, Discover, American Express accepted)

Name ————————————————————

Address ————————————————————

City, State, Zip ————————————————

Phone ————————————————————

Email _____

# Order directly from Hannibal Books

***Now My Eye Sees You*** by Greg Ammons. A late-in-life, first-time
father, though seminary-trained and a pastor for many years, gains unfath-
omable understanding about God when his son is born.

_____ copies at $12.95 =_____

***Daughter of No One*** by Viola Palmer. A young girl living on the border
of Nicaragua and Honduras is shipped off to work in a Honduran sweatshop.
He journey home and to Christ is a riveting read, especially for ages 8-12.

_____ copies at $14.95 = _____

***Way Back in the Country*** by Kay Moore. Country recipes from six
generations of an East Texas farm family encourage other families to pre-
serve their own lore through cooking stories.

_____ copies at $9.95 = _____

***Rebekah Ann Naylor, M.D.*** by Camille Lee Hornbeck. When
Rebekah Ann Naylor responds to God's call to be a missionary physician,
she becomes the first woman to graduate from the surgical residency program at her medical school and goes on to establish a hospital in India.

_____ copies at $19.95 = _____

***The Man in the Green Jeep*** by Viola Palmer. Global missions is per-
sonalized through this captivating glance into children's lives and culture in
Central America.

_____ copies at $9.95 = _____

Add $3 postage and handling for the first book, 50 cents for each additional book.

Shipping & handling: _____

Texas residents add 8.25% sales tax: _____

Total enclosed (check or money order): _____

Name_____

Address_____

City_____State_____Zip_____

Phone _____ Email _____

*See address and other contact information on page 301.*